MAUI
THE BOOK OF

A whimsical island guide that includes "secret" recipes from Maui's chefs, illustrated maps, the best restaurants and unusual stories of what to do and where to go.

By Kenneth & Beverly Stilwell

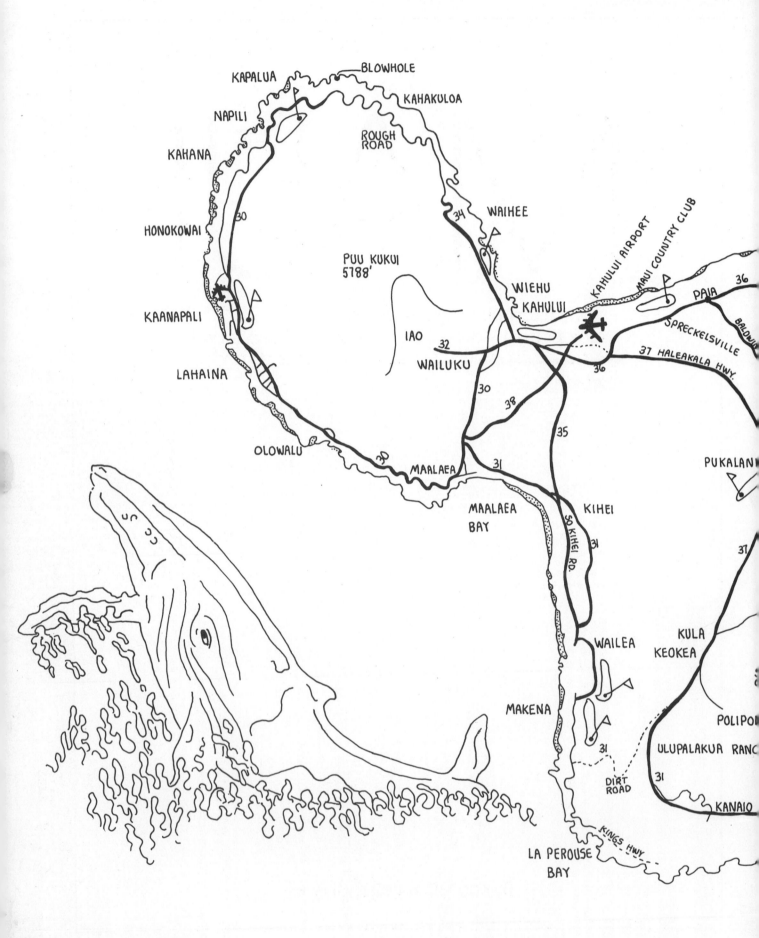

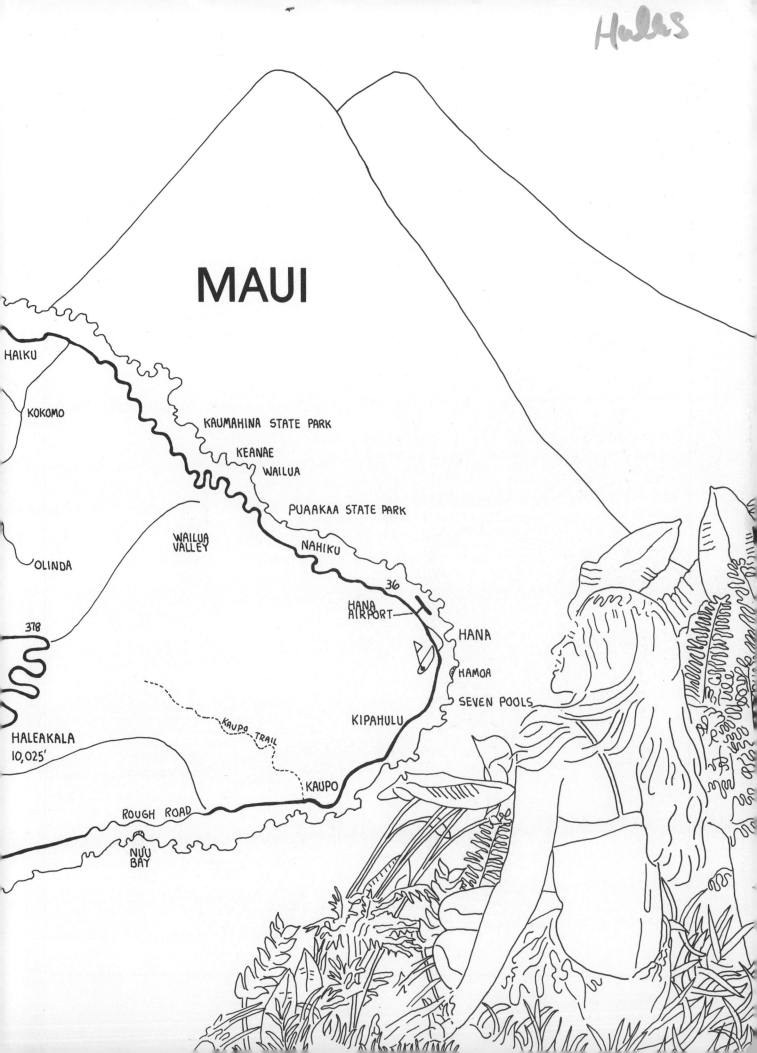

THE
BOOK
OF
MAUI

Illustrations by Kenneth Stilwell

chuck Jumot
1983

Lollipop Press,
Maui

MADE AND PUBLISHED IN MAUI
BY LOLLIPOP PRESS
BOX 309
KIHEI, MAUI, HAWAII 96753
PUBLISHER AND EDITOR: KENNETH AND BEVERLY STILWELL
ASSISTANT TO EDITOR: NICOLE DONAHUE
PHOTOGRAPHIC GRAPHICS: DEXTER SOARES
ADVERTISING SALES: LAURIE HAYES KENNEDY
FOUNDER: LAHL E. POHPPE

CONTENTS

(GENERAL CONTENTS)

SECTION ONE: IAO, HALEAKALA, HANA
SECTION TWO: KIHEI, WAILEA
SECTION THREE: LAHAINA
SECTION FOUR: KAANAPALI
SECTION FIVE: NAPILI-KAPALUA

RESTAURANTS-ALPHABETICAL INDEX
HOW TO USE THIS BOOK

CONTENTS BY SECTION

SECTION ONE
   MAPS
   INTRODUCTION
   MAPS (CENTRAL MAUI)
   IAO VALLEY
   UP COUNTRY
   MAP (UP COUNTRY)
   PUKALANI-MAKAWAO
   HALEAKALA
   KULA
   MAP (KULA AND BEYOND)
   ULUPALAKUA
   TO PAIA
   PAIA
   TO HANA
   MAP (TO HANA)
   KEANAE-WAILUA
   HANA
   MAP (HANA)
   BEYOND HANA
   MAP (BEYOND HANA)
   SEVEN POOLS-KIPAHULU-KAUPO

CONTENTS

SECTION TWO: KIHEI, WAILEA
   MAPS
   INTRODUCTION
   MAALAEA
   KIHEI
   MAP (KIHEI)
   WAILEA
   MAP (WAILEA)
   BEYOND WAILEA (MAKENA)
   MAP (BEYOND WAILEA)
   TO LAHAINA (MAP)

SECTION THREE: LAHAINA
   MAPS
   INTRODUCTION
   ACTIVITIES
   LAHAINA RESTORATION FOUNDATION

SECTION FOUR: KAANAPALI
   MAPS
   INTRODUCTION
   ACTIVITIES
   MAP (HONOKOWAI, KAHANA)

SECTION FIVE: NAPILI, KAPALUA
   MAPS
   INTRODUCTION
   NAPILI
   KAPALUA BAY
   BEYOND KAPALUA
   MAP (BEYOND KAPALUA)
   KAHAKULOA

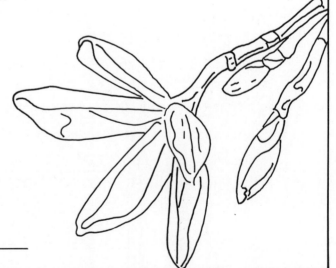

RESTAURANTS IN ALPHABETICAL ORDER   S= SECTION

ALEX'S HOLE IN THE WALL   S3 LAHAINA

AMBROSIA   S2 WAILEA SHOPPING VILLAGE

BLACK ROCK TERRACE   S4 KAANAPALI (SHERATON)

CHEZ PAUL   S3 OLOWALU

DISCOVERY ROOM   S4 KAANAPALI (SHERATON)

DON THE BEACHCOMBER   S4 KAANAPALI (ROYAL LAHAINA)

EL CRABCATCHER   S4 KAANAPALI (WHALER'S VILLAGE)

HOTEL HANA MAUI DINING ROOM   S1 HANA

KAPALUA BAY CLUB   S5 (KAPALUA RESORT)

KAPALUA BAY HOTEL DINING ROOM S5 (KAPALUA RESORT)

KIMO'S   S3 LAHAINA

KULA LODGE   S1 HALEAKALA HIGHWAY 377 BEFORE 378 TURN-OFF

LA FAMILIA   S1 WAILUKU

LA PEROUSE   S2 WAILEA (HOTEL INTER CONTINENTAL MAUI)

LONGHI'S   S3 LAHAINA

MAMA'S FISH HOUSE   S1 PAST PAIA TOWARDS HANA

MING YUEN   S1 KAHULUI

MOBY DICK   S4 KAANAPALI (ROYAL LAHAINA)

MONOCO RESTAURANT   S5 NAPILI (NAPILI SHORES RESORT)

PALM COURT   S2 WAILEA (WESTIN WAILEA BEACH)

PEACOCK   S4 KAANAPALI (2650 KEKAA DR.)

PLANTATION VERANDA   S5 (KAPALUA RESORT)

POLLI'S   S1 MAKAWAO

PUKALANI TERRACE   S1 PUKALANI GOLF COURSE CLUBHOUSE

QUEE QUEEG   S4 KAANAPALI (MAUI SURF)

RAFFLE'S   S2 WAILEA (WESTIN WAILEA BEACH)

RESTAURANT OF THE MAUI MOON   S5 NAPILI (NAPILI KAI)

ROBAIRE'S   S2 KIHEI

SPATS II   S4 KAANAPALI (HYATT REGENCY)

SWAN COURT   S4 KAANAPALI (HYATT REGENCY)

TIKI TERRACE   S4 KAANAPALI (KAANAPALI BEACH HOTEL)

WATERFRONT   S2 MAALAEA (MILOWAI CONDOMINIUMS)

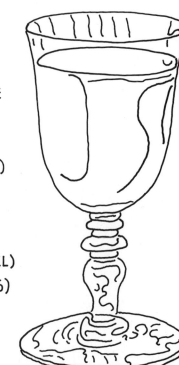

PROTEA

ALOHA! WELCOME TO MAUI!
DO YOU WANT TO FIND THE BEST OF MAUI? THE BEST SHOPS?
THE BEST RESTAURANTS? ONLY THE BEST? THEN USE THE
BOOK OF MAUI, THE LOCAL, SELECTIVE GUIDE!

WE LIVE HERE! WE LOVE MAUI! DO YOU WANT TO KNOW
THE MAUI THAT We KNOW? WE CAN MAKE YOUR TIME
HERE QUALITY TIME! YOU CAN WASTE A LOT OF TIME
HERE WITHOUT A MAUI FRIEND TO SHOW YOU AROUND!

THERE IS SO MUCH TO SEE AND DO HERE! MORE THAN
YOU COULD HAVE IMAGINED? BUT PERHAPS LIKE
US YOU HAVE YEARS TO DISCOVER MAUI? NO?
THEN PLEASE TAKE US ALONG! YOU WON'T
FIND ALL OF MAUI IN OUR BOOK- NONE OF
THE PLASTIC OR IMITATION MAUI IS IN-
CLUDED (EVEN PARADISE ISN'T PERFECT)
JUST THE BEST OF
MAUI! MAUI NO
KA OI!

SCOTCH MIST

THE BOOK OF MAUI MAILED FREE!

HAVE THE BOOK OF MAUI MAILED DIRECT TO YOUR HOME! POSTPAID! OR HAVE A *real* "MADE-IN-MAUI GIFT" SENT TO A FRIEND OR RELATIVE. POSTPAID! YOUR FRIENDS WHO DO NOT HAVE THE BOOK OF MAUI OR WHO HAVE NEVER VISITED MAUI WILL RECEIVE A TASTE OF THE *real* MAUI! SEND $12.95 ONLY; WE PAY SPECIAL 4TH CLASS POSTAGE AND YOUR NAME AND ADDRESS (AND YOUR FRIEND'S NAME AND ADDRESS IF A GIFT) TO: BOOK OF MAUI, P.O. BOX 309, KIHEI, MAUI, HI. 96753. FOR FIRST CLASS POSTAGE ADD $2 PER COPY. GUARANTEED.

FREE POSTAGE!

OUR ADVERTISERS

WE STAND BEHIND THE PRODUCTS AND SERVICES OF OUR ADVERTISERS. AS YOU WILL NOTICE, THE BOOK OF MAUI IS NOT JUST AN EXCUSE FOR ADVERTISING COPY! WE STRIVE TO PRESENT OUR CLIENTS TO YOU IN AN HONEST, REFRESHING AND EFFECTIVE MANNER, AND IN RETURN WE EXPECT THEM TO GUARANTEE THEIR PRODUCTS AND SERVICES! OUR ADVERTISERS ARE THE FINEST SHOPS, RESORTS, HOTELS, ETC., ON MAUI, BUT SHOULD A PROBLEM EVER ARISE, WE *will* HELP YOU! WRITE: CUSTOMER SERVICE DEPT., THE BOOK OF MAUI, P.O. BOX 309, KIHEI, MAUI, HI., 96753.

TRAVEL PLANS

WHO COULD BETTER ADD QUALITY TO YOUR MAUI TRAVEL PLANS FOR NEXT YEAR, THAN THE BOOK OF MAUI? WANT CURRENT INFORMATION ON CONDOS AND HOTELS AND CAR RENTALS HERE ON MAUI? INFORMATION ON TOURS, AIRLINES AND SPECIAL ACTIVITIES? LET BOOK OF MAUI HELP YOU WITH OUR QUALITY, MADE-IN-MAUI TRAVEL PLANS! FROM SUGGESTIONS TO RESERVATIONS! $10 ONE-TIME SERVICE CHARGE. WRITE: TOURISM DEPT., THE BOOK OF MAUI, P.O. BOX 309, KIHEI, MAUI, HAWAII, 96753.

HUMUHUMUNUKUNUKUAPUAA ~ FISH!

HOW TO USE THE BOOK OF MAUI

MAUI HAS MANY DIMENSIONS: FROM THE OCEAN-BOTTOM TO THE CRATER OF HALEAKALA; FROM THE ULTRA-RESORT LIFE OF KAPALUA TO THE ULTRA-ISLAND LIFE OF KAUPO. AND A VISITOR FINDS ENDLESS INFORMATION ABOUT IT ALL! SHOPS. HOTELS. RESORTS. CONDOMINIUMS. ACTIVITIES. SERVICES. SIGHTS. SPORTS. TOURS. BEACHES. RESTAURANTS. CAFES. NIGHTSPOTS. AND MORE SHOPS. MORE RESTAURANTS! VERY CONFUSING!

WITH A LIMITED TIME ON MAUI HOW CAN YOU EVER HOPE TO FIND WHAT IS TRULY BEST? WHAT *are* THE BEST SHOPS, THE BEST RESTAURANTS, THE BEST ACTIVITIES, THE BEST SIGHTS? AND WHERE ARE THEY? AND HOW DO I FIND THEM? HOW DO I KEEP FROM WASTING MY TIME? MANY VISITORS NEVER *really* SEE MAUI BECAUSE OF THIS CONFUSION AND LACK OF RELIABLE, SELECTIVE INFORMATION. THIS IS SAD, BECAUSE MAUI TRULY IS ONE OF THE WORLD'S SPECIAL PLACES!

THE SECTIONS

THE BOOK OF MAUI BRINGS ORDER TO ALL THE CONFUSION! IT DIVIDES THE ISLAND INTO 5 SECTIONS: #1, IAO, HALEAKALA, HANA; #2, KIHEI, WAILEA; #3, LAHAINA; #4 KAANAPALI; AND #5, NAPILI, KAPALUA.
WITHIN EACH SECTION WE HAVE SELECTED THE BEST SHOPS, RESTAURANTS, SIGHTS AND ACTIVITIES. AND WE USE MANY, MANY MAPS! IF WE TELL YOU ABOUT SOMETHING, WE MAKE SURE YOU CAN EASILY AND QUICKLY FIND IT!

CAREFULLY FOLLOW THE BOOK OF MAUI THROUGH EACH SECTION AND YOU WILL EXPERIENCE MAUI! WITH NO CONFUSION OR WASTE OF TIME YOU TRULY WILL FIND THE BEST OF MAUI! MAUI IS A SPECIAL WORLD AND ONLY OUR MADE-IN-MAUI GUIDE TRULY BRINGS IT TO YOU!

RESTAURANTS AND RESTAURANT/CHEFS' RECIPES

THE BOOK OF MAUI HAS CAREFULLY SELECTED THE BEST RESTAURANTS OF MAUI! MANY ARE AMONG HAWAII'S BEST! MANY ARE EVEN "WORLD-CLASS"! YOU MAY FIND SOME WELL-KNOWN NAMES ABSENT FROM OUR LIST, BUT FOR THIS YEAR WE BELIEVE THIS TO BE AN ACCURATE PRE-   SENTATION OF MAUI'S BEST RESTAURANTS!

RECIPES? RECIPES IN A GUIDE BOOK? WELL, yes!
THESE ELEGANT BUT SIMPLE CHEFS' RESTAURANT RECIPES ARE, IN THEMSELVES, A TOUR OF MAUI'S FINEST RESTAURANTS AND THEIR CUISINE! THESE RECIPES ARE NOT FRIVOLOUS! THEY ARE THE SERIOUS CREATIONS OF MAUI'S FINEST CHEFS, PERSONALLY PROVIDED TO THE BOOK OF MAUI. THESE RECIPES REALLY ARE INCREDIBLE TREASURES OF MAUI! POSSIBLY SOME OF THE BEST GIFTS YOU COULD TAKE BACK HOME! TRY THEM OUT IN YOUR MAUI KITCHEN!

AND WHEN YOU ARE HOME AGAIN AND IN YOUR OWN KITCHEN, OUR FRIENDLY LITTLE BOOK OF MAUI WILL BECOME YOUR SPECIAL AND GENUINE... MAUI COOKBOOK!

THE BOOK OF MAUI

SECTION ONE
IAO TO HALEAKALA

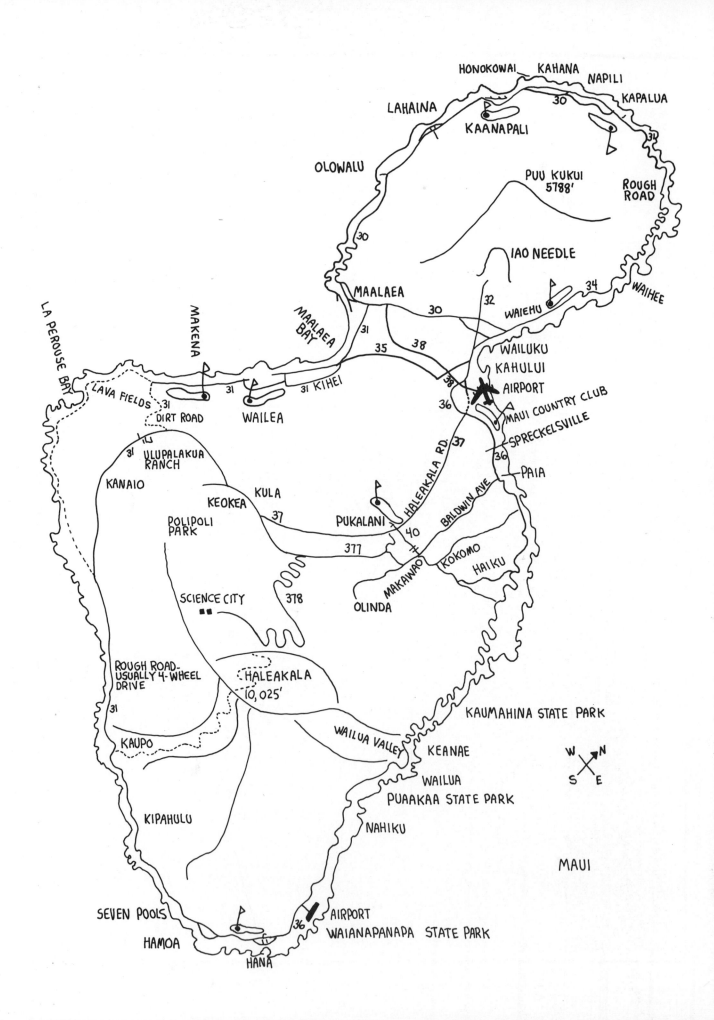

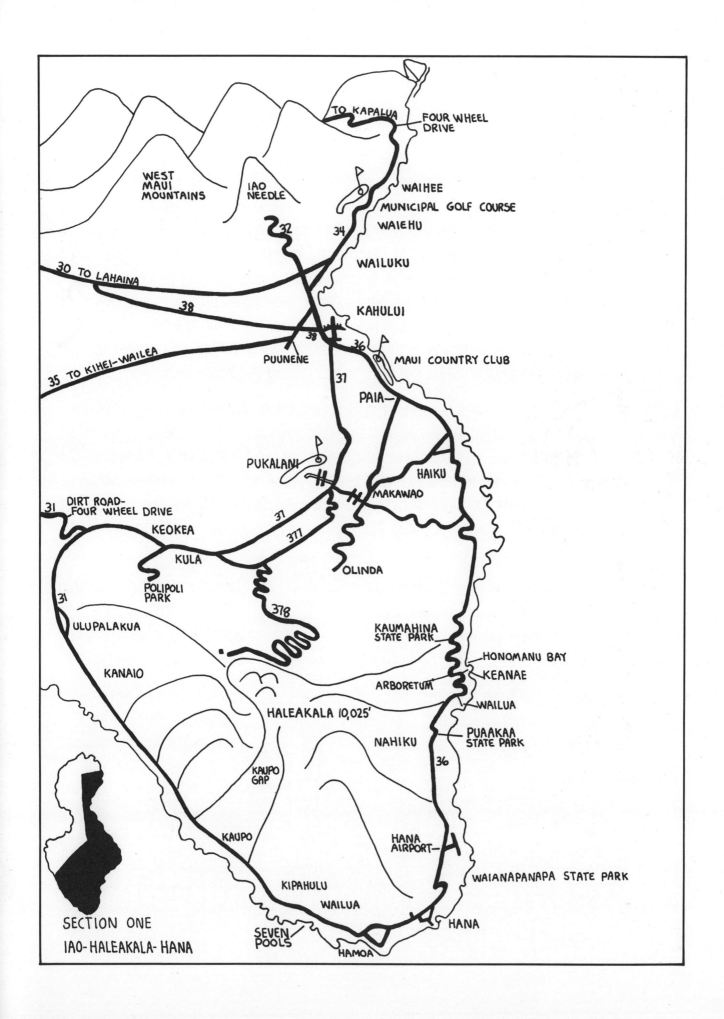

TO KAPALUA — FOUR WHEEL DRIVE

WEST MAUI MOUNTAINS

IAO NEEDLE

WAIHEE

MUNICIPAL GOLF COURSE

WAIEHU

32

34

30 TO LAHAINA

38

WAILUKU

KAHULUI

38

36

35 TO KIHEI-WAILEA

PUUNENE

MAUI COUNTRY CLUB

37

PAIA

PUKALANI

HAIKU

HALEAKALA 10,025'

MAKAWAO

31

DIRT ROAD- FOUR WHEEL DRIVE

KEOKEA

37

KULA

377

OLINDA

POLIPOLI PARK

31

378

ULUPALAKUA

KAUMAHINA STATE PARK

HONOMANU BAY

KANAIO

KEANAE

ARBORETUM

WAILUA

PUAAKAA STATE PARK

NAHIKU

36

KAUPO GAP

KAUPO

HANA AIRPORT

WAIANAPANAPA STATE PARK

KIPAHULU

WAILUA

HANA

SECTION ONE
IAO- HALEAKALA- HANA

SEVEN POOLS

HAMOA

SECTION ONE

IAO VALLEY. UP COUNTRY. HALEAKALA. HANA. SEVEN POOLS.

GEOGRAPHICALLY, THIS IS THE LARGEST, MOST DRAMATIC, AND JUST POSSIBLY THE MOST BEAUTIFUL SECTION OF MAUI. THERE ARE MANY INTERESTING LOCAL SHOPS IN WAILUKU, KAHULUI, MAKAWAO, PAIA AND HANA. SEVEN RESTAURANTS ARE WORTHY OF YOUR TIME AND MONEY: LA FAMILIA IN WAILUKU; MING YUEN IN KAHULUI; PUKALANI TERRACE IN PUKALANI; POLLI'S IN MAKAWAO; KULA LODGE, ON THE WAY TO HALEAKALA; MAMA'S FISH HOUSE, JUST PAST PAIA AT KUAU; AND OF COURSE, THE DINING ROOM IN THE HOTEL HANA MAUI! THERE ARE FOUR GOLF COURSES: WAIEHU; MAUI COUNTRY CLUB; PUKALANI; AND HANA. HORSEBACK RIDING IS AVAILABLE FOR KULA, HALEAKALA AND HANA. THE BEST BEACHES ARE AT HANA. THIS SIDE OF MAUI IS NOT NOTED FOR ITS BEACHES ALTHOUGH THERE ARE INTERMITTANT SANDY BEACHES FROM WAIEHU PAST PAIA, MANY OF WHICH ARE QUIET AND UNDEVELOPED. THE BEST SURF IS AT HOOKIPA BEACH PARK.

THIS COULD BE CALLED THE WORKING SIDE OF MAUI. COUNTY AND STATE OFFICES ARE LOCATED IN WAILUKU, AT THE ENTRANCE TO THE IAO VALLEY. HERE YOU WILL GLIMPSE THE REMNANTS OF AN OLD, PROVINCIAL MAUI TOWN. KAHULUI IS THE BUSY, COMMERCIAL CENTER OF MAUI. THE WHOLE TOWN WAS BURNED TO THE GROUND IN 1900 BECAUSE OF THE PLAGUE, AND IN 1942 KAHULUI WAS EVEN SHELLED BY JAPANESE SUBMARINES! KAHULUI IS MAUI'S PORT CITY FOR THE EXPORT OF SUGAR, MOLASSES AND PINEAPPLE AND FOR THE "IMPORT" OF ABOUT 2,000,000 YEARLY VISITORS!

FOR A TOUR OF THE SECTION TAKE HIGHWAY 32 THEN TAKE HIGHWAY 34 BEYOND WAILUKU ALONG A QUIET AND CHARMING DRIVE, WHICH BECOMES TO KAPALUA) AND IS BEST COMPLETED WITH A INTO THE BEAUTIFUL IAO VALLEY. THE COAST TO WAIHEE. THIS IS QUITE ROUGH (ON THE WAY VERY STURDY VEHICLE!

TAKE HIGHWAY 36 (THE HANA HIGHWAY) TO YOU UP INTO THE FERTILE UP-COUNTRY, THE THE MIGHTY HALEAKALA. THIS IS THE LAND OF HIGHWAY 37. THIS WILL CARRY FLORID AND LUSH SLOPES OF FARMS AND RANCHES, RAISING

WAILUKU SUGAR MILL

EVERYTHING FROM PROTEA AND ORCHIDS TO CATTLE AND QUARTERHORSES. OUR LOCAL VEGETABLES ARE GROWN HERE, INCLUDING THE LUSCIOUS "KULA ONION"- WHICH IS AS NEAR AS AN ONION CAN COME TO BEING A FRUIT! MAKAWAO IS A HAWAIIAN-WESTERN TOWN. KULA IS NOT SO MUCH A TOWN AS A "REGION OF GROWING" ABOVE KIHEI AND WAILEA. PAIA WAS BUILT AROUND THE FIRST SUGAR CANE MILL ON MAUI. TAKE HIGHWAY 40 LEFT FROM HIGHWAY 37, IN PUKALANI, TO GO TO MAKAWAO. YOU MAY REACH PAIA FROM MAKAWAO BY FOLLOWING BALDWIN AVENUE ALL THE WAY TO THE HANA HIGHWAY (36) (A PLEASANT DRIVE THROUGH THE PINEAPPLE FIELDS) OR YOU MAY RETURN TO THE HIGHWAYS 36 AND 37 JUNCTION, AND TURN RIGHT ONTO 36. FOR HALEAKALA, TURN LEFT JUST PAST PUKALANI ONTO 377, WHICH WILL PLEASANTLY WIND YOU TO 378, WHERE YOU TURN LEFT. HAVE SOMETHING WARM TO SLIP ON WHEN YOU FINALLY GET TO THE TOP! BOTH HIGHWAYS 377 AND 37 WEND YOU THROUGH KULA. BEYOND KULA, 37 CARRIES YOU SPECTACULARLY ABOVE THE OCEAN TO TEDESCHI WINERY AND ULUPALAKUA RANCH.

FROM PAIA TO HANA ON HIGHWAY 36, THE EXQUISITE ROAD TO HANA, ARE ENDLESS CURVES AND WATER-FALLS! THERE ARE VIEWS OF THE TARO-BANANA GROWING REGIONS OF KEANAE AND WAILUA. HANA, ON THE EASTERN SIDE OF THE VOLCANO, IS A PARADISE STILL ISOLATED FROM THE OUTSIDE WORLD. NO HIGH-RISES HERE, JUST COTTAGES, TROPICAL FORESTS AND THE SEA. BEYOND HANA IS KIPAHULU, WHERE CHARLES LINDBERG IS BURIED. HERE TOO, ARE THE FAMOUS AND BEAUTIFUL SEVEN POOLS. IF YOU HAVE FOUR-WHEEL DRIVE YOU CAN CONTINUE ON AROUND THIS SOUTH SIDE OF HALEAKALA TO WAILEA RESORT (SECTION TWO) (TAKE THE DIRT ROAD TO MAKENA, 31); IF NOT, YOU MUST RETURN TO KAHULUI ON THE HANA HIGHWAY, 36. TURN LEFT AT HIGHWAY 38(0). FOLLOW SIGNS TO KIHEI-WAILUA, SECTION TWO.

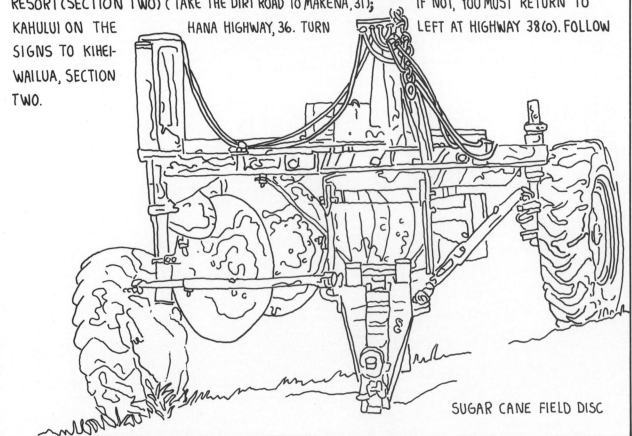

SUGAR CANE FIELD DISC

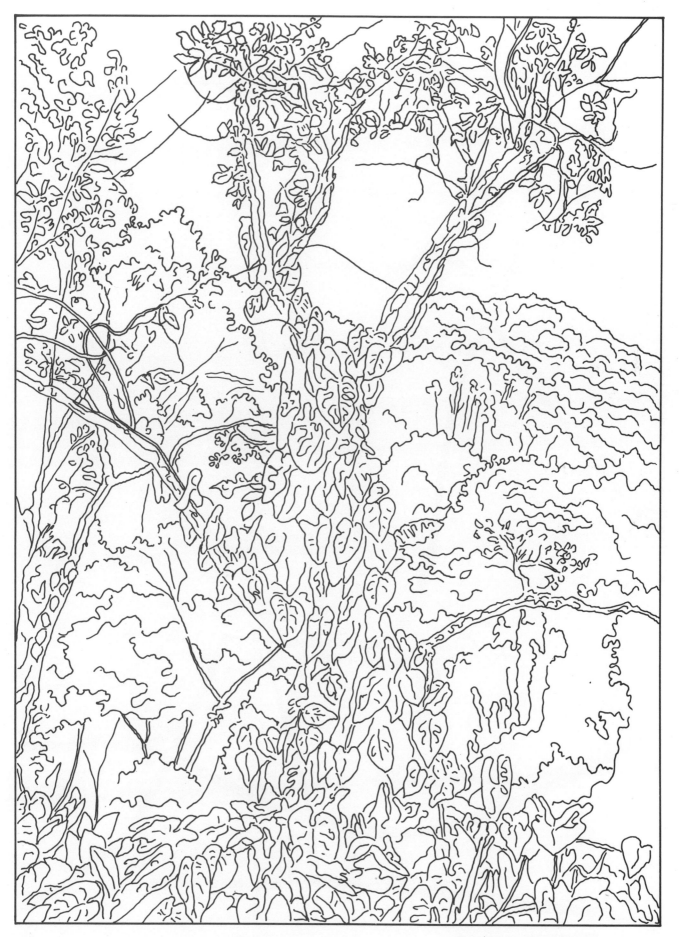

WEST MAUI MOUNTAINS

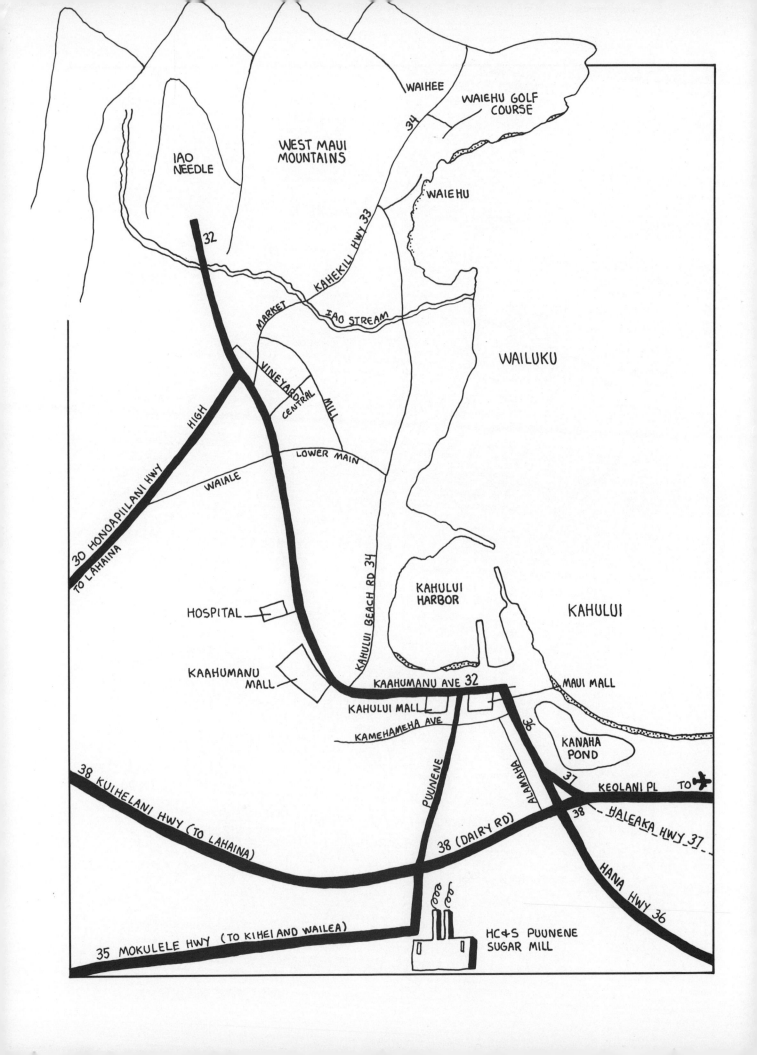

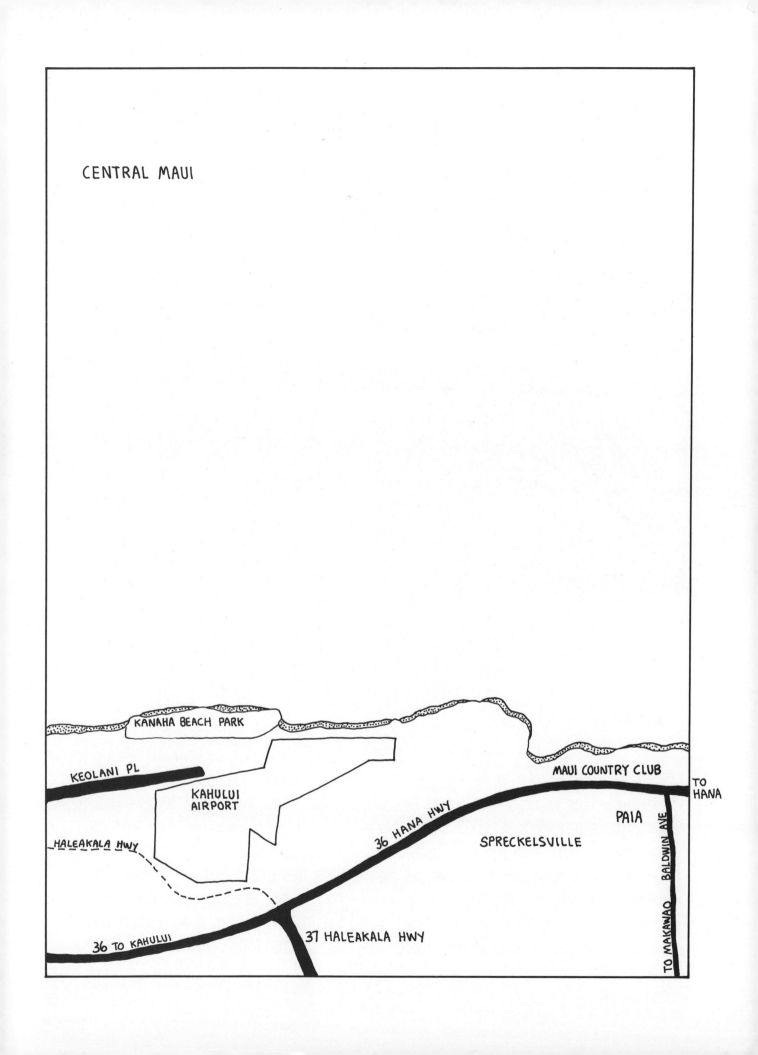

IAO VALLEY
"THE NEEDLE"

TO REACH THE VALLEY TAKE   THE MAIN STREET THROUGH WAILUKU, HIGHWAY
32. THERE ARE SIGNS SHOWING YOU THE WAY IN. DON'T RUSH, THE WHOLE VALLEY HAS CHARM,
NOT JUST THE FAMOUS NEEDLE! LOVELY KEPANIWAI PARK IS MIDWAY ON THE SHORT DRIVE
UP VALLEY. MARK TWAIN CALLED IAO VALLEY THE 'LITTLE YOSEMITE' OF HAWAII, WHICH IS
ABSURD! WHY COMPARE IT? IAO HAS ITS OWN BEAUTY, ITS STEEP PALI, ITS GREEN GROWTH
OF FERNS AND MOSS, CLOUDS AND BIRDS, AND OF COURSE, THE NEEDLE, WHICH FOR SOME
REASON IS ACCLAIMED AS THE FOCAL POINT OF THE VALLEY. THE NEEDLE IS AN ERODED VOLCANIC
MONOLITH WHOSE TIP IS 2250 FEET ABOVE SEA-LEVEL BUT ONLY 1200 FEET (IF THAT, DEPENDING

UPON SOME ARTFUL MEASURING!) ABOVE THE VALLEY FLOOR. OTHER SPECTACULAR CLIFFS TOWER ABOVE IT AND ARE JUST AS BEAUTIFUL!

FOR A LOCAL, THE NEEDLE IS NOT THAT INTERESTING, REALLY. CERTAINLY IT IS WORTH A VISIT. BUT THE THING TO DO IS TAKE THE MANDATORY GAZE AT THE NEEDLE AND THEN WALK DOWN TO IAO STREAM AND FOLLOW THE PATHS UPSTREAM! IT IS UP IN THE HIGH VALLEY THAT YOU CAN SENSE THE MAUI OF OLD. LINGER AWHILE. DON'T BE IN A RUSH! SIT AND LISTEN TO THE THOUSANDS OF BIRDS, WATCH THE EVER-CHANGING MIST ON THE PALI (CLIFFS), EXAMINE THE FLOWERS, CATCH THE SCENT OF THE VALLEY AS IT IS BORNE TO YOU BY THE GENTLE WINDS. IF YOU ARE USING THIS BOOK AS YOUR SELECT GUIDE OF MAUI AND IAO IS PERHAPS YOUR FIRST "STOP," PLEASE DO USE YOUR TIME IN IAO VALLEY TO SLOW DOWN AND GET THE *feel* OF MAUI. MAUI IS MORE THAN A MERE VISUAL EXCURSION! IT IS ALSO A JOURNEY OF THE HEART, AND WHEN YOUR *heart* SEES MAUI, YOU WILL HAVE "ENCHANTMENT" AS WELL AS BEAUTY!

MAUI LOVES TO TELL YOU ITS SECRETS, BUT OFTENTIMES IT WHISPERS, SO YOU MUST LISTEN VERY CAREFULLY TO THE ENCHANTING TALES! HISTORY, OF COURSE, MAY NOT BE SO "ENCHANTING" AS THE PAST REMEMBERS THAT IT WAS IN THIS VOLCANIC CUL-DE-SAC THAT KING KAMEHAMEHA AND HIS HAOLE (WHITE) ADVISERS USED CANNON

IAO STREAM

KEPANIWAI PARK

TO DESTROY THE DEFENDING ARMY OF MAUI. WHEN THE BATTLE WAS ENDED IAO STREAM WAS
GLUTTED WITH WARRIORS' BODIES AND KAMEHAMEHA HAD TAKEN ANOTHER STEP TOWARDS
HIS GOAL OF RULING OVER ALL OF THE ISLANDS. THE KING OF MAUI AND HIS DEFEATED MEN
ESCAPED DEATH BY FLEEING ON FOOT ACROSS THE RUGGED WEST MAUI MOUNTAINS THROUGH
THE OLOWALU GAP TO LAHAINA. KEPANIWAI PARK ("DAMMING OF THE WATERS"), WITH ITS
LITTLE POOLS AND GARDENS, IS SYMBOLIC OF THE GREAT BATTLE, ALTHOUGH IT WAS BUILT AS AN
ETHNIC TRIBUTE TO THE SEVERAL RACES WHICH HAVE CREATED THE MAUI OF TODAY.

Resort
By William Welsh
© 1979 William Welsh
Paper Moon Graphics, Inc.

fantasea

exquisite fashions, gifts,
jewelry, cards & toys
— *in the Maui style.*

21 Market Street   Wailuku, Maui   Telephone: 242-9561

LA FAMILIA RESTAURANT

TWO LOCATIONS

2119 VINEYARD STREET
WAILUKU
SERVING LUNCH AND DINNER
11:30AM - 9PM MONDAY - SATURDAY
244-7281
MEXICAN; STEAKS AND SEAFOOD

KIHEI KAI NANI VILLAGE
2511 SO. KIHEI ROAD
KIHEI
BREAKFAST, LUNCH, DINNER
8AM - 10PM DAILY
879-8824
MEXICAN FOOD

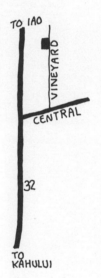

LA FAMILIA RESTAURANT

SOUR CREAM CHICKEN ENCHILADA

2	OZ	BUTTER
1		FOUR-OUNCE CAN GREEN CHILES (CHOPPED)
1/2		ONION
1/4	t	SALT
1	t	CUMIN
1/2	t	CAYENNE
2	T	FLOUR
1		CUP CHICKEN BROTH
1		4-5 POUND CHICKEN (COOKED, DE-BONED, SHREDDED)

OIL (TO FRY)
HALVED TORTILLAS (CORN OR FLOUR)
SOUR CREAM (TOPPING)

1. IN A LARGE SKILLET WITH MELTED BUTTER, SAUTE GREEN CHILES AND ONIONS FOR 2-3 MINUTES.
2. ADD SEASONINGS.
3. SHAKE FLOUR AND CHICKEN BROTH TOGETHER IN A JAR AND ADD IT TO THE MIXTURE.
4. ADD COOKED CHICKEN AND BLEND WELL. SET ASIDE.
5. IN ANOTHER SKILLET OF HOT OIL FRY HALVED TORTILLAS QUICKLY (2-3 SECONDS EACH SIDE).
6. PLACE CHICKEN MIXTURE INSIDE EACH TORTILLA. ROLL, SERVE WITH WHITE SAUCE (SEE NEXT RECIPE) AND A TABLESPOON OF SOUR CREAM ON TOP!

COOKING TIME: 12-15 MINUTES
(DOES NOT INCLUDE COOKING
TIME FOR CHICKEN)
SERVES: FOUR (10-12 ENCHILADAS)

LA FAMILIA RESTAURANT

WHITE SAUCE (FOR SOUR CREAM CHICKEN ENCHILADA)

4	OZ BUTTER
1/4	CUP FLOUR
2-1/2	CUPS MILK
1	FOUR-OUNCE CAN GREEN CHILES (CHOPPED)
1/4	CUP SALSA
1/2 t	SALT
1 t	CUMIN
1/2 t	CAYENNE PEPPER

1. IN A MEDIUM SAUCE PAN MELT BUTTER, ADD FLOUR TO MAKE A ROUX.
2. SLOWLY POUR IN MILK AND BRING TO A BOIL.
3. ADD REMAINING INGREDIENTS AND SIMMER WHILE PREPARING ENCHILADAS.

PREPARATION: 5 MINUTES
COOKING: 15 MINUTES

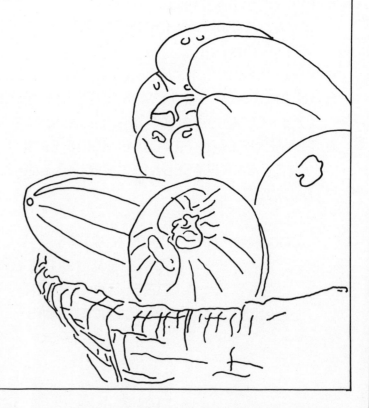

HALE HOIKEIKE, THE HISTORICAL MUSEUM, IS ON THE IAO ROAD JUST BEFORE TURNING INTO THE VALLEY. HALE HOIKEIKE, BUILT IN 1832, WAS ONCE PART OF THE WAILUKU FEMALE SEMINARY. THE MUSEUM IS WORTH A SHORT VISIT. HERE YOU WILL LEARN ABOUT PETROGLYPHS (STONE WRITING) AND VIEW RELICS OF MAUI'S REGAL PAST.

MING YUEN

明苑

THE CHINESE RESTAURANT

CANTONESE CUISINE
SZECHUAN SPECIALTIES

LUNCH 11-2 MONDAY-SATURDAY
DINNER 5-9 DAILY
871-7787
162 ALAMAHA PLACE
KAHULUI

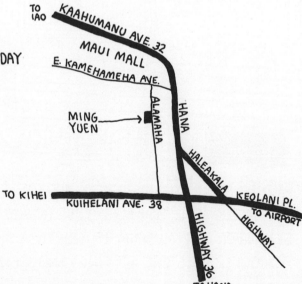

HOT MA PO TOFU

MING
YUEN

1/2   LB. TOFU (HALF INCH CUBES)
1   T VEGETABLE OIL
2   OZ. GROUND PORK (COARSE)
1/2   t GARLIC (FINELY CHOPPED)
1/4   t FRESH GINGER (FINELY CHOPPED)
1   T CHILI PASTE (FOUND IN DELICATESSENS)
1   T SHERRY WINE (DRY)
3/4   CUP FRESH CHICKEN STOCK
1   T OYSTER SAUCE
1   T SOY SAUCE
1   T SESAME OIL
1   T SUGAR
1   HEAPING t CORNSTARCH MIXED WITH 1 T WATER.
1   T GREEN SCALLIONS (FINELY CHOPPED)

1. HEAT WOK 'TILL HOT. POUR IN ONE T OIL.
2. ADD PORK AND FRY UNTIL COLOR STARTS TO CHANGE.
3. ADD GARLIC, GINGER, CHILI PASTE AND SHERRY. FRY FOR 5-10 SECONDS.
4. ADD CHICKEN STOCK, OYSTER SAUCE, SOY SAUCE, SESAME OIL AND SUGAR.
5. BRING TO BOIL AND SLIGHTLY THICKEN WITH CORNSTARCH MIXTURE.
6. ADD TOFU CUBES JUST BEFORE SERVING, STIRRING GENTLY UNTIL TOFU
   IS HEATED THOROUGHLY.
7. SERVE ON LARGE PLATTER AND GARNISH WITH GREEN SCALLIONS.

PREPARATION: 10-12 MINUTES
COOKING: 7-10 MINUTES
SERVES: 4

MING YUEN

STEAMED WHOLE FISH WITH
GINGER AND SCALLIONS

1-1/2 LBS FRESH FISH FOR STEAMING-LIKE SNAPPER
SALT AND PEPPER (TO TASTE)
OIL (TO COAT PLATTER)
1/2   CUP SCALLIONS (CUT INTO ONE-INCH PIECES)
1/4   CUP FRESH GINGER (FINE, ONE-INCH STRIPS)
1   T VEGETABLE OIL
1/2   CUP CHICKEN STOCK
3/4   CUP SOY SAUCE
1   t SESAME OIL
CILANTRO (TO GARNISH)

1. WITH A SHARP KNIFE CUT FISH ONE-HALF INCH DEEP ALONG BOTH SIDES OF VERTICAL FIN.
2. SEASON FISH WITH SALT AND PEPPER
3. PUT OIL IN CENTER OF PLATTER (ENOUGH TO ACCOMODATE THE FISH).
4. PLACE HALF OF SCALLIONS AND GINGER ON THE PLATTER.
5. PLACE FISH ON THIS BED OF SCALLIONS AND GINGER.
6. PLACE IN A CHINESE STEAMER AND STEAM FOR 12 MINUTES OR UNTIL MEAT CAN
   BE DETACHED FROM THE BONE.
7. REMOVE PLATTER FROM STEAMER. PLACE REMAINING SCALLIONS AND GINGER ON FISH.
8. HEAT OIL IN WOK UNTIL VERY HOT. POUR OIL OVER THE LENGTH OF FISH.
9. BRING STOCK AND SOY SAUCE TO BOIL. ADD SESAME OIL. POUR OVER FISH.
   GARNISH WITH FRESH SPRIGS OF CILANTRO.

PREPARATION: 7-10 MINUTES
COOKING: 15-20 MINUTES
SERVES: 4

Maui ❀ Mall

Maui's neighborly shopping mall. Thirty-eight shops to please you. Drugs, sundries, photography, clothing, shoes, supermarket, books, jewelry, tobacco, flowers, sewing needs, snacks, hairdresser, records, restaurants, souvenirs and much, much more! Ample free parking. Free entertainment on weekends. Just a 5-minute drive from Kahului Airport on Kaahumanu Avenue (Highway 32). Beautifully landscaped with large trees and colorful plants.

The Petroglyph Garden covers 1100 sq. ft. at the east end of the Maui Mall, and includes four major groups of boulders weighing from three to eight tons each. Every boulder has several rock carvings. Bring your camera.

Petroglyph sites are believed to indicate areas where a weary traveler might find refuge. In the center of the Petroglyph Garden, a large monkey pod tree offers its shade and comfort to those who stop to enjoy this bit of Old Hawaii.

AFTERNOON AT KAHULUI MALL

THE UP COUNTRY

THIS IS THE BEAUTIFUL LAND OF RANCHES AND ORCHIDS, PANIOLOS (COWBOYS) AND PROTEA, CARNATIONS AND REDWOODS, HUNTING AND HORSEBACK RIDING! IT IS EASILY REACHED VIA HIGHWAY 37, THE HALEAKALA HIGHWAY, WHICH CUTS THROUGH MILES OF SUGAR CANE FIELDS. THE FIRST TOWN ON YOUR WAY UP IS PUKALANI, A QUIET AND

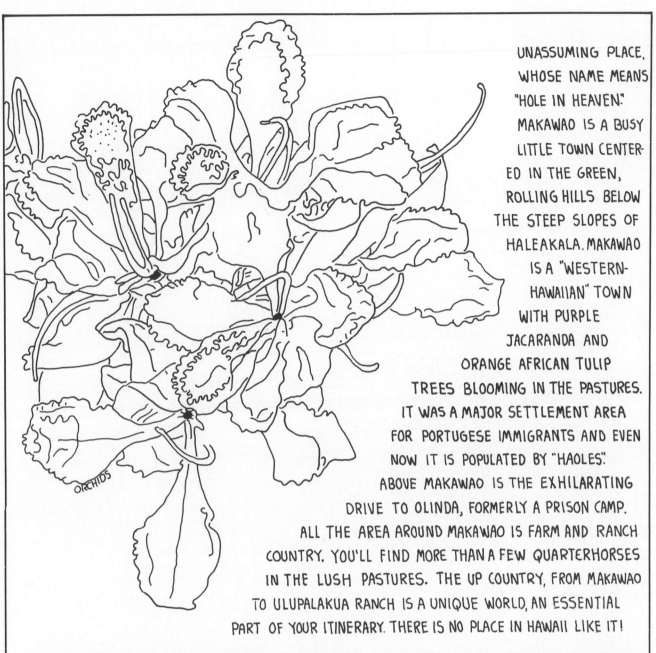

ORCHIDS

UNASSUMING PLACE, WHOSE NAME MEANS "HOLE IN HEAVEN." MAKAWAO IS A BUSY LITTLE TOWN CENTERED IN THE GREEN, ROLLING HILLS BELOW THE STEEP SLOPES OF HALEAKALA. MAKAWAO IS A "WESTERN-HAWAIIAN" TOWN WITH PURPLE JACARANDA AND ORANGE AFRICAN TULIP TREES BLOOMING IN THE PASTURES. IT WAS A MAJOR SETTLEMENT AREA FOR PORTUGESE IMMIGRANTS AND EVEN NOW IT IS POPULATED BY "HAOLES". ABOVE MAKAWAO IS THE EXHILARATING DRIVE TO OLINDA, FORMERLY A PRISON CAMP. ALL THE AREA AROUND MAKAWAO IS FARM AND RANCH COUNTRY. YOU'LL FIND MORE THAN A FEW QUARTERHORSES IN THE LUSH PASTURES. THE UP COUNTRY, FROM MAKAWAO TO ULUPALAKUA RANCH IS A UNIQUE WORLD, AN ESSENTIAL PART OF YOUR ITINERARY. THERE IS NO PLACE IN HAWAII LIKE IT!

SCENTED BY EUCALYPTUS AND SPRUCE, KULA, AT 3000 FEET IS THE CENTER OF THE FLOWER AND VEGETABLE GROWING ON MAUI. BE SURE TO TAKE BOTH 377 AND 37, PLUS MANY OF THE SIDE-ROADS. WHEN YOU GET OFF THE HIGHWAYS, WHO KNOWS WHAT YOU WILL FIND? EXOTIC PROTEA GARDENS? FIELDS OF CARNATIONS AND ORCHIDS? KULA BOTANICAL GARDENS, OFF OF 377, HAS OVER 700 DIFFERENT PLANTS (INCLUDING PROTEA). POLIPOLI SPRINGS (TAKE POLIPOLI RD OFF OF 37), PART OF THE KULA GAME RESERVE, REQUIRES AN ASCENT OF SOME 3000 FEET. POLIPOLI IS THE 6500' CINDER CONE UP-SLOPE AS YOU DRIVE ON 37 TOWARDS ULUPALAKUA RANCH. THE ROAD IS SEVERAL MILES OF DIRT (STURDY VEHICLES ONLY), BUT IT IS SPECTACULAR and IT LEADS YOU TO 280 ACRES OF REDWOOD TREES! PAST KULA IS THE OLD MAKEE MILL WHERE SUGAR WAS REFINED UNTIL 1880. IT IS NOW ULUPALAKUA RANCH, A WORKING CATTLE RANCH. THIS IS A RUSTIC, LOVELY AND INTERESTING AREA ON THE SOUTHWESTERN SLOPE OF HALEAKALA, OVERLOOKING MAKENA AND KAHOOLAWE.

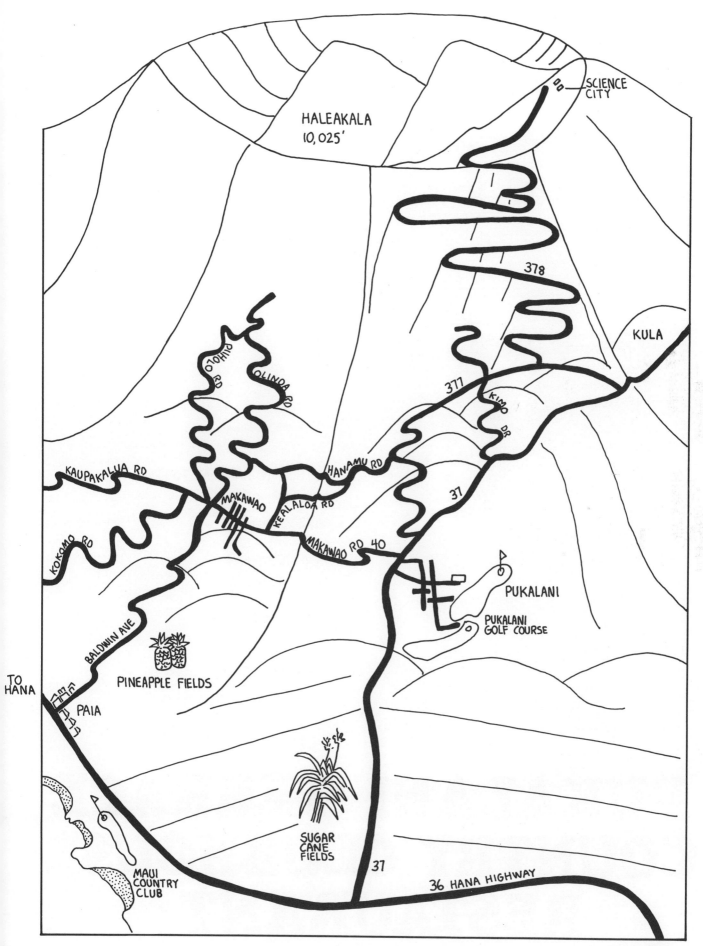

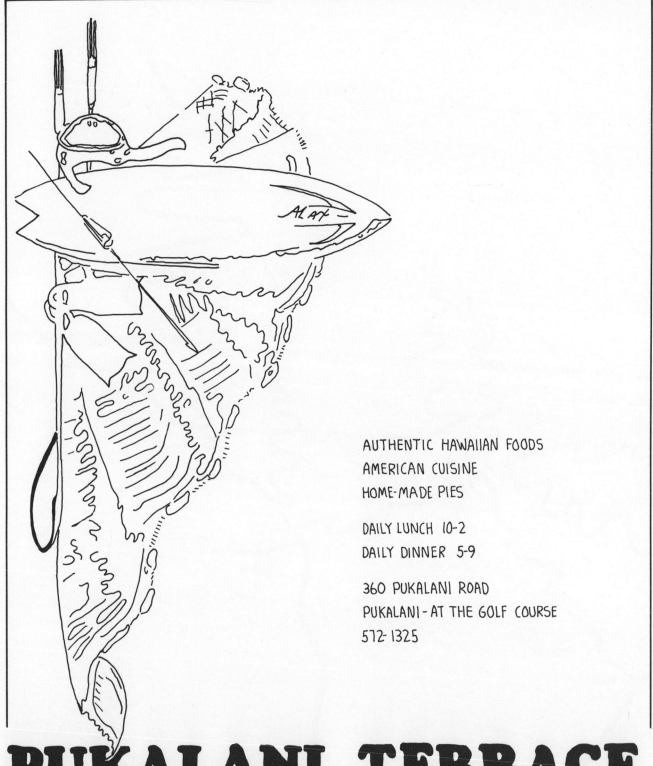

AUTHENTIC HAWAIIAN FOODS
AMERICAN CUISINE
HOME-MADE PIES

DAILY LUNCH 10-2
DAILY DINNER 5-9

360 PUKALANI ROAD
PUKALANI - AT THE GOLF COURSE
572-1325

PUKALANI TERRACE COUNTRY CLUBHOUSE RESTAURANT

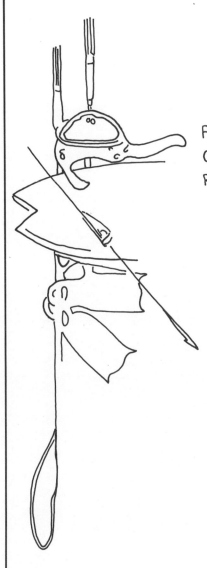

PUKALANI TERRACE
COUNTRY CLUBHOUSE
RESTAURANT

LAU LAU

1	LB BEEF CUBED (SMALL)
1	LB PORK
1	t SALT
8	TARO LEAVES (SUBSTITUTE SPINACH)
8	TI LEAVES (SUBSTITUTE CORN HUSKS OR BANANA LEAVES)

1. MIX MEATS WITH SALT. DIVIDE INTO 8 PORTIONS.
2. WRAP EACH PORTION IN A TARO LEAF AND THEN WRAP IN TI LEAF. TIE ENDS TOGETHER.
3. PLACE IN STEAMER. COVER WITH FOIL. STEAM 2 HOURS.
4. SERVE WITH POI OR RICE.

PREPARATION: 45 MINUTES
COOKING: 2 HOURS
SERVES: 4

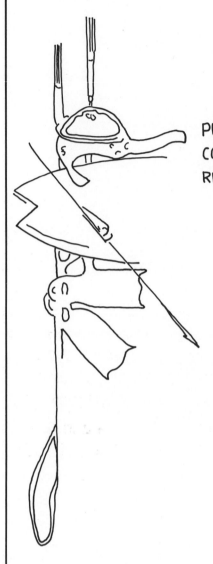

PUKALANI TERRACE
COUNTRY CLUBHOUSE
RESTAURANT

PIPI KAULA

2   LBS BEEF (RED STEAK) CUT INTO
      2" X 1" STRIPS
OIL FOR FRYING
3   CLOVES OF GARLIC (MINCED FINE)
1   t BLACK PEPPER
1   CUP SHOYU SAUCE (SOY SAUCE)

1. MARINATE BEEF IN SHOYU, GARLIC AND PEPPER OVERNIGHT.
2. DRAIN LIQUID IN MORNING AND "SUN DRY" HALF A DAY (TWO AND
   ONE-HALF HOURS EACH SIDE).
3. CHILL AND SLICE THINLY.
4. IN A LARGE SKILLET, FRY BEEF IN HOT OIL UNTIL BROWN
   (6-7 MINUTES EACH SIDE).

PREPARATION: 10 MINUTES, PRIOR TO MARINATING
COOKING: 12-15 MINUTES
SERVES: 4

MAUI IS A STORY OF AGRICULTURE. EVEN NOW MAKAWAO TO KULA IS AN AREA DOMINATED BY SUGAR CANE, PINEAPPLE, FLOWER CROPS AND VEGETABLES. SUGAR CANE HAS PROVIDED A LIVING FOR A MAJORITY OF ISLANDERS FOR MANY DECADES BUT IT WOULD APPEAR THAT ITS BEST DAYS ARE IN THE PAST. PINEAPPLE GROWING ON MOLOKAI IS ENDING AND IT IS AN OPEN QUESTION AS TO WHETHER PINEAPPLE'S FUTURE ON LANAI AND MAUI IS SECURE. A DECLINE IN THESE VITAL INDUSTRIES AND THE PROBABLE BOOM IN MAUI TOURISM WILL BRING SIGNIFICANT SOCIAL CHANGE TO MAUI IN THE DECADE AHEAD.

BUT MAUI HAS NOT BEEN MERELY A STORY OF SUGAR AND PINEAPPLE. COFFEE WAS GROWN ON THE VOLCANIC SLOPES OF HALEAKALA BUT ONLY ON THE KONA SIDE OF HAWAI'I DID IT BECOME SUCCESSFUL. POTATOES WERE ONCE A BIG CROP FOR KULA, AND AT ONE TIME MAKAWAO WAS SURROUNDED BY GREAT WHEAT FIELDS! THERE WAS EVEN A FLOUR MILL IN TOWN. THIS WHEAT BOOM DIED AS THE ENDLESS FIELDS OF THE MAINLAND MIDWEST CAME INTO PRODUCTION.

IN WAILUKU MULBERRY GROVES WERE PLANTED. SILK WORMS FROM CHINA WERE IMPORTED FOR SILK CULTURE. DROUGHT AND SPIDERS DESTROYED THE EFFORT. COTTON WAS AN IMPORTANT CROP FOR 30 YEARS, ESPECIALLY DURING THE U.S. CIVIL WAR WHEN THE NORTH'S SUPPLY OF COTTON WAS CUT OFF. 1867-87 WERE PEAK RICE-GROWING YEARS. RICE WAS PLANTED IN UP-ROOTED TARO PATCHES. OTHER GROWING EFFORTS WERE MADE WITH ORANGES, BANANAS, OLIVES AND TOBACCO BUT BY MID-CENTURY THE SHIFT WAS TO SUGAR CANE, MAUI'S MOST PRODUCTIVE CROP!

GINGER

MAUI BEAVERS AT WORK

HALEAKALA RANCH

ESTABLISHED IN THE 1870s AS PI'IHOLO PLANTATION,
A SUGAR CANE PLANTATION IN THE HEART OF MAKAWAO, HALEAKALA RANCH
IS MAUI'S LARGEST - STRETCHING FROM KULA TO KIHEI. SINCE WORLD WAR I
IT HAS OPERATED AS A CATTLE RANCH, PRIVATELY OWNED BY THE BALDWIN CLAN.

POLLi'S

Mexican
Restaurant

A MEATLESS MEXICAN MENU

LUNCH 11:30-2 MON-SAT
DINNER 5:30-10 DAILY
SUNDAY BRUNCH 10:30-2:30

1202 MAKAWAO AVE
MAKAWAO
572-7808

VEGGIE TAMALEN

POLLI'S

DOUGH (MASA)

1-1/2 CUPS SOY OIL
4-1/2 CUPS CORN MASA
2-1/2 t SALT
2-1/2 CUPS WARM WATER
1   CUP DICED JALAPEÑO PEPPERS
3   DZ. CORN HUSKS*

FILLING

18   LARGE FRESH GREEN CHILES (THREE 7-OZ. CANS)
2   LBS JACK CHEESE (SLICED INTO 36 PIECES)
2   SLICED ONIONS

1. MIX DOUGH INGREDIENTS WITH WOODEN SPOON. COVER. SET ASIDE.

continued...

POLLI'S

2. (CONTINUED) SOAK APPROXIMATELY
   THREE DOZEN CORN HUSKS IN WATER
   UNTIL SOFT.
   *(NOTE: TO THOSE UNFAMILIAR WITH
   CORN HUSKS- THEY ARE NOT UNIFORM
   IN SIZE AND YOU MAY NEED TO USE
   TWO IF HUSKS ARE NARROW. CORN
   HUSKS MAY BE PURCHASED IN A
   DELI OR A MEXICAN SHOP.)
   WHEN HUSKS ARE SOFT, DRAIN AND DRY.

3. DRAIN CANNED CHILES OR ROAST AND
   PEEL FRESH CHILES, CUT IN HALF.

4. TAKE CORN HUSK IN LEFT HAND.
   SPREAD TWO T. OF MASA (DOUGH),
   FROM LEFT SIDE (HALFWAY UP) TO
   MIDDLE. SEE ILLUSTRATION.

5. PLACE HALF CHILE, CHEESE SLICE AND
   ONE T. OF ONION IN CENTER OF MASA.

6. ROLL HUSK TIGHTLY (STARTING
   FROM LEFT AND FOLD DOWN TOP.

7. PLACE TAMALES FOLDED-SIDE DOWN
   IN STEAMER.

8. STEAM 3 HOURS. CHECK WATER
   LEVEL FREQUENTLY.

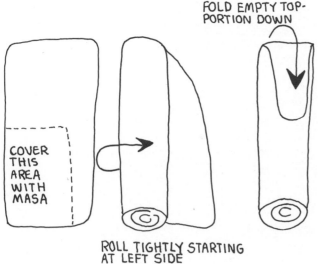

FOLD EMPTY TOP-
PORTION DOWN

COVER
THIS
AREA
WITH
MASA

ROLL TIGHTLY STARTING
AT LEFT SIDE

PREPARATION: 2 HOURS
STEAMING: 3 HOURS
MAKES 3 DOZEN

THE MAKAWAO RODEO

A BUSY RODEO CIRCUIT MAY NOT FIT YOUR IMAGE OF MAUI, BUT THE ANNUAL MAKAWAO RODEO IS ONLY ONE OF TEN-FOURTEEN OFFICIALLY SANCTIONED RODEOS HELD EACH YEAR IN HAWAII! THE MAKAWAO RODEO IS THE BIGGEST. IT IS ORGANISED BY THE MAUI ROPING CLUB AND HAS BEEN HELD ON THE

FOURTH OF JULY WEEKEND FOR 28 YEARS. COMPETITION LASTS FOR THREE DAYS. THE HAWAIIAN RODEO CIRCUIT IS "AMATEUR" BUT IT IS RECOGNIZED BY THE MAIN-LAND. GENERALLY 250-300 RIDERS FROM HAWAII, THE MAINLAND, CANADA AND AUSTRALIA PARTICIPATE.

KULA LODGE

ON THE HALEAKALA HIGHWAY (377) BEFORE
THE 378 TURN-OFF

AMERICAN CUISINE
DAILY BREAKFAST 7:30-11
DAILY LUNCH 11-2:30
DAILY DINNER 5:30-9 (EXCEPT TUESDAY)
878-1535

KULA LODGE

POACHED FISH
ORIENTAL STYLE

2		LBS FISH (WHITE-ONO-ULUA-PAPIO ETC.)
1		CLOVE GARLIC (MINCED)
1	t	FRESH GINGER (GRATED)
1	t	GREEN ONIONS
2	T	SHOYU (SOY SAUCE)
2	T	SUGAR
2	T	HOT PEANUT OR SESAME OIL

1. POACH FISH IN BOILING SALTED WATER FOR APPROXIMATELY 15 MINUTES.
2. PLACE FISH ON SERVING PLATE AND SPRINKLE WITH GARLIC, GINGER AND GREEN ONIONS.
3. POUR SHOYU MIXED WITH SUGAR OVER FISH.
4. TO SEAL IN ALL FLAVORS, POUR HOT OIL OVER FISH.

PREPARATION: 5 MINUTES
COOKING: 15-18 MINUTES
SERVES: ONE

KULA LODGE

RUM CAKE

1   CUP CHOPPED NUTS (YOUR CHOICE)
1   DUNCAN HINES YELLOW CAKE MIX
1   PKG (3-3/4 OZ) VANILLA PUDDING
4   EGGS (BEAT ONE AT A TIME)
1-1/2 CUPS COLD WATER
1/2   CUP DARK RUM (80 PROOF)

GLAZE

1/4   LB. BUTTER
2   OZ. WATER
1   CUP SUGAR
4   OZ. RUM

1. GREASE AND FLOUR 10-INCH TUBE PAN.
2. SPRINKLE NUTS ON BOTTOM OF PAN.
3. MAKE CAKE BATTER OUT OF REST OF INGREDIENTS. POUR OVER NUTS.
4. BAKE ONE HOUR AT 350 DEGREES. COOL. INVERT ON PLATE.
5. PREPARE GLAZE:

1. MELT BUTTER IN SAUCEPAN. STIR IN WATER AND SUGAR.
2. BOIL, STIRRING CONSTANTLY 2-3 MINUTES.
3. REMOVE FROM HEAT AND STIR IN RUM.
4. DRIZZLE GLAZE OVER TOP OF CAKE AND OVER THE SIDES. ALLOW CAKE TO
   ABSORB GLAZE. REPEAT UNTIL GLAZE IS USED UP.

PREPARATION: 15-20 MINUTES
BAKING/ COOKING: 1 HOUR / 5-7 MINUTES
YIELDS: ONE 10-INCH TUBE CAKE.

*Escape on the wings
of the butterfly.
For an hour. For a day.*

Escape to the wonders of Haleakala at sunrise, or the dramatic cliffs of Molokai at sunset. The beauty of Hawaii is captured best in the luxury of a Papillon aerial excursion. A feast of sight and sound, often combined with a quiet picnic at a secluded touch-down point await you on our fine selection of flights.

Rainbows, waterfalls and courteous service abound each flight. Our locations are convenient, our experience incomparable. Enjoy Hawaii at its finest, with Papillon Helicopters.

Papillon
Helicopters

For information and reservations,
on Maui, call 669-4884
and on Kauai, call 826-6591.

HALEAKALA

THE "HOUSE OF THE SUN" DOMINATES EAST MAUI. THE ROAD TO THE TOP OF THIS VOLCANO TAKES YOU FROM ZERO TO 10,000 FEET IN JUST 40 MILES, THE ONLY (PAVED) ROAD IN THE WORLD TO GET YOU SO HIGH SO FAST! ALLOW YOURSELF AT LEAST THREE HOURS TO MAKE YOUR ASCENT (HANA HIGHWAY, 36, TO HIGHWAY 37, THROUGH PUKALANI; AT PUKALANI JUNCTION, TURN LEFT ON 377, WHICH WILL TAKE YOU TO 378, THE HALEAKALA HIGHWAY). HAVE BREAKFAST BEFOREHAND OR STOP AT KULA LODGE ON YOUR WAY UP. BRING A PICNIC LUNCH AND SOME WARMER CLOTHES!

TEN MILES FROM THE TOP AT ABOUT 7000 FEET, IS THE RALPH S. HOSMER GROVE WHERE THE CLEAR MOUNTAIN AIR IS SCENTED WITH PINE, SPRUCE AND EUCALYPTUS TREES! ABOVE THE GROVE IS KALAHAKU OVERLOOK, WHOSE VIEW SHOULD NOT BE PASSED-BY! AND FINALLY THE RIM OF THE CRATER, ONE OF THE GREATEST VIEWING-POINTS ANYWHERE! THE SUMMIT IS A 360° PANORAMA OF THE BIG ISLAND, KAHOOLAWE, LANAI, MOLOKAI, AND FLOATING IN THE FAR, FAR DISTANCE, OAHU!

WITHIN THE CRATER ARE 30 MILES OF TRAILS WHICH CAN EASILY BE TRAVERSED BY FOOT OR BY HORSE. FOR OVERNIGHT TRIPS, IF YOU HAVE PLANNED IT WELL IN ADVANCE WITH PARK RANGERS, YOU CAN STAY IN A WELL-EQUIPPED CABIN- CAMPING FOR A NIGHT INSIDE A VOLCANO! HALEAKALA IS NOT ACTIVE, BUT AS IT IS WITH ANY DORMANT VOLCANO, IT COULD BECOME ACTIVE AT ANY TIME! THE MOST RECENT EXCITEMENT WAS APPARENTLY IN 1790, ON THE SOUTHEAST SIDE, SOUTH OF MAKENA IN THE KINAU REGION.

HALEAKALA AND ITS ETERNAL CLOUDS! THIS WONDERFUL SIGHT IS BEST AT DAWN, BEST PHOTO-GRAPHED BEFORE NOON. AN ASCENT OF HALEAKALA VIA HELICOPTER (PAPILLON IS VERY GOOD) WILL PROVIDE YOU WITH AN EXCITING EXPERIENCE!

PROTEA

ALONG THE CHAIN OF HAWAIIAN ISLANDS ABOUT FOUR THOUSAND FEET ABOVE THE BLUE PACIFIC, UP IN THE SWIRLING MISTS OF HALEAKALA VOLCANO, NESTLED AMIDST ROCK GARDENS AND WATERFALLS, LIE SIXTEEN ACRES OF EXOTIC PROTEA PLANTS. THIS IS PROTEA GARDENS OF MAUI. SIX DEDICATED PEOPLE TEND OVER 10,000 PLANTS IN THIS UNIQUE GROWING ENVIRONMENT HIGH ON A VOLCANO'S SLOPES.

THE RICH SOIL, WARM DAYS AND COOL NIGHTS OF KULA MAKE THIS ONE OF THE MOST IMPORTANT PROTEA GROWING REGIONS ON EARTH! DUE TO THE ELEVATION AND CONSTANT CLOUD COVER HERE ARE GROWN THE FINEST PROTEA, WITH THE DEEPEST COLORS AVAILABLE IN THE WESTERN WORLD!

PROTEA WERE FIRST INTRODUCED ONTO HALEAKALA'S SLOPES IN 1965 AND BEGAN TO BE COMMERCIALLY EX-PORTED IN 1975. THE SEEDS TAKE FROM A MONTH TO TWO years TO GERMINATE AND GROW INTO BUSHES UP TO SIX FEET IN HEIGHTH. PROTEA IS THE prestige PLANT WITH GORGEOUS BLOSSOMS OF NEARLY A FOOT ACROSS ON ONE VARIETY! PROTEA ARE SOME OF THE MOST UNUSUAL CUT-FLOWERS YOU WILL EVER SEE! FRESH PROTEA LAST FOR WEEKS IN WATER AND LAST FOR YEARS DRIED.

WE THINK YOU WOULD ENJOY A BOUQUET OF FRESH OR DRIED MAUI PROTEA (BY MAIL-ORDER, $25 AND UP) FROM PROTEA GARDENS OF MAUI. THE BOOK OF MAUI GUARANTEES A HIGH QUALITY PRODUCT!

KULA

THE EXCELLENT GROWING REGION OF
KULA- CERTAINLY ONE OF THE WORLD'S
BEST- IS NOW FAMOUS FOR MANY CROPS, INCLUDING
PROTEA, ORCHIDS AND *maui* ONIONS. MAUI ONIONS
ARE AS NEAR TO BEING A FRUIT AS AN ONION WILL EVER
COME! A GOOD MAUI RESTAURANT MUST SERVE THIS
SWEET AND CRISP MAUI- OR KULA- ONION !

HIGH ABOVE MAALAEA BAY ON THE SLOPES OF MIGHTY
HALEAKALA, KULA WAS NEVERTHELESS INVOLVED
WITH WHALING! WHALERS LIKED POTATOES. THE
WHALING CAPTAINS BROUGHT SEED POTATOES
AND THE TRADERS SAW TO IT THAT THEY BECAME
POTATO FIELDS. KULA BECAME A GREAT POTATO
PATCH, TEN MILES LONG, A MILE WIDE! SHIPS SAILED
INTO MAALAEA BAY, RAISED A WHITE FLAG WHICH WAS
EASILY SEEN UP-SLOPE AT KULA. AT THIS SIGNAL THE
POTATOES WERE DUG, PUT IN BARRELS AND CARRIED,
WITH OTHER PRODUCE, DOWN THROUGH THE DRY KIAWE
BRUSHLANDS TO THE WAITING SHIPS. KULA'S POTATO
DAYS ENDED WHEN THE DROUGHT OF 1851 DESTROYED MOST
OF THE CROP! KULA HAS HAD AN INTERESTING PAST AND
IT IS A BEAUTIFUL REGION TODAY, CERTAINLY REASON
ENOUGH TO EXPLORE IT CAREFULLY! DON'T RUSH!

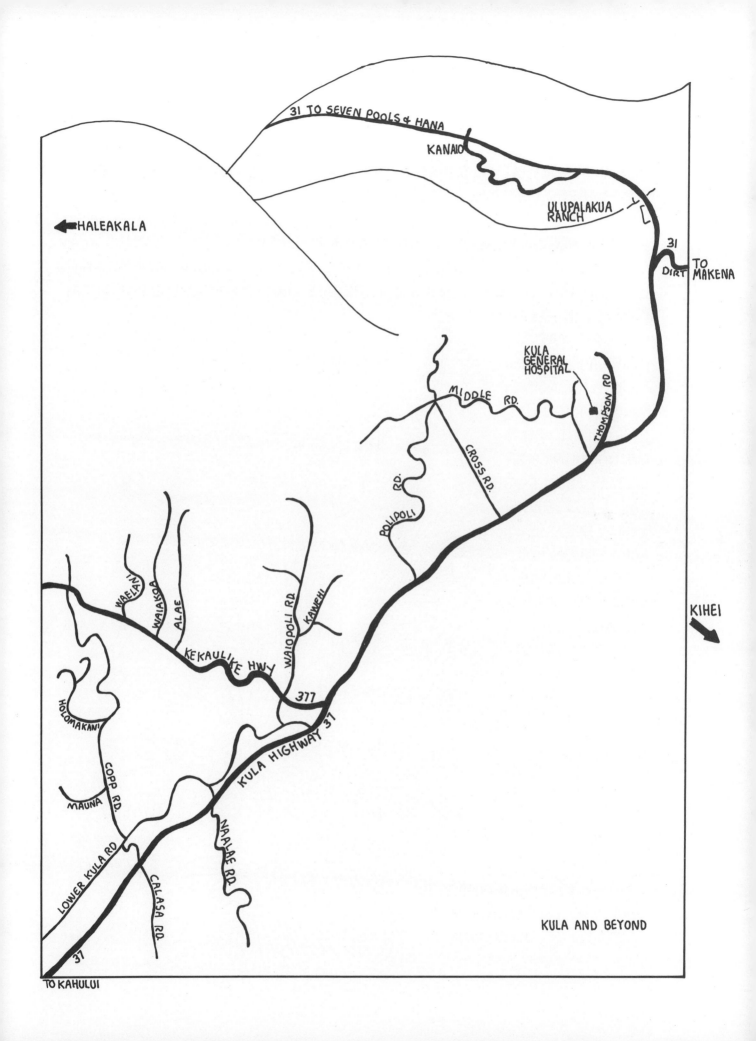

31 TO SEVEN POOLS & HANA

KANAIO

HALEAKALA

ULUPALAKUA
RANCH

31
DIRT
TO
MAKENA

KULA
GENERAL
HOSPITAL

MIDDLE RD.

CROSS RD.

THOMPSON RD.

POLIPOLI
RD.

POLIPOLI

KIHEI

WAELANI

WAIAKOA

ALAE

WAIOPOLI RD.

KAWEHI

KEKAULIKE HWY

377

KULA HIGHWAY 37

HOLOMAKANI

COPP RD.

MAUNA

LOWER KULA RD.

CALASA RD.

NAALAE RD.

37

TO KAHULUI

KULA AND BEYOND

ULUPALAKUA

JAMES MAKEE WAS A RICH HONOLULU MERCHANT WHO BEGAN RAISING CATTLE
AT ULUPALAKUA ON THE SLOPES OF HALEAKALA IN 1855. FIVE YEARS LATER
THE PASTURES CONTAINED SUGAR CANE. MAKEE PLANTED 1000 ACRES OF CANE,
BUILT A MANSION OVERLOOKING KAHOOLAWE AND LANAI, GUEST HOUSES, A
VILLAGE FOR LABORERS, A CHURCH, A JAIL, A BILLIARD PARLOR, A BOWLING ALLEY...
AND A SUGAR MILL! THE PROCESSED SUGAR WAS CARTED DOWN-SLOPE TO MAKENA,
ULUPALAKUA'S SEAPORT. FOR A FEW YEARS "ROSE RANCH" WAS THE LARGEST SUGAR
COMPLEX IN HAWAII,
UNTIL A GREAT
HURRICANE LEVELLED
EVERY PLANT. A DROUGHT
FOLLOWED, KILLING
EVERY PLANT STILL
LIVING! ULUPALAKUA
TODAY IS AGAIN A CATTLE
RANCH AND TEDESCHI
WINERY AND VINE-
YARD ENTICES YOU
WITH A PINEAPPLE
WINE SOLD FROM THE
OLD JAIL!

WILD POPPIES IN
THE LAVA FIELDS-
ULUPALAKUA

KAHULUI TO PAIA

THE KANAHA BIRD SANCTUARY, BETWEEN
KAHALUI AND THE AIRPORT, BETWEEN THE OCEAN
AND THE HANA HIGHWAY, 36, WAS BUILT IN THE
1700s AS A ROYAL FISHPOND. IT IS NOW A
NATIONAL HISTORIC LANDMARK, A HOME FOR
MANY HAWAIIAN BIRDS (SUCH AS HERONS AND
PLOVERS) AS WELL AS AN IMPORTANT
MIGRATORY STOP FOR WATERFOWL FROM
AS FAR AWAY AS CANADA AND ALASKA.
FEW VISITORS EVER NOTICE THIS IMPORTANT REFUGE AS THEY RUSH BY
ON THEIR WAY TO HANA OR HALEAKALA, SO YOU'LL HAVE THESE BEAUTIFUL
BIRDS ALL FOR YOURSELF! BEST VIEWED FROM THE JUNCTION OF 36 AND 396.

SPRECKELSVILLE, WHOSE BUILDINGS HAVE
BEEN TORN DOWN, WAS ONCE A SUGAR
CANE PLANTATION TOWN CREATED
BY CLAUS SPRECKELS, THE "SUGAR
KING OF HAWAII". SPRECKELS
CULTIVATED THOUSANDS OF
ACRES OF SUGAR CANE AND
BUILT THE BEST SUGAR MILL IN
THE WORLD. SPRECKELS WAS
A MAJOR POLITICAL FIGURE-HE
EVEN TRIED TO RESTORE QUEEN
LILIUOKALANI TO THE THRONE IN
1893. MAUI COUNTRY CLUB IS THE
SITE OF ONCE-PROSPEROUS SPRECKELSVILLE.

SPRECKELSVILLE BEACH IS UNDEVELOPED, WITH SOME
GOOD BEACHCOMBING AND FINE VIEWS OF THE WEST MAUI
MOUNTAINS. H.A. BALDWIN PARK IS THE MOST POPULAR
BEACH PARK ON THIS THE WINDWARD SIDE OF THE ISLAND;
BETWEEN SPRECKELSVILLE AND PAIA. THE PARK HAS
MANY FACILITIES, EVEN A BASEBALL FIELD, BUT THE REAL
ATTRACTION IS THE LONG SURF. BALDWIN IS POPULAR
FOR BODYSURFING-AND ON OCCASION- BOARD SURFING.

PAIA

PAIA IS A SLEEPY LITTLE COASTAL TOWN WHERE BALDWIN & ALEXANDER BUILT THEIR FIRST SUGAR CANE PLANTATION, WATERING THE CANE FIELDS BY MEANS OF AN AQUADUCT WHICH CARRIED WATER FROM HALEAKALA'S WETTEST SLOPES. THE MILL IS STILL IN OPERATION. BUT NOW PAIA REACHES OUT TO THE HANA-BOUND TOURISTS RUSHING THROUGH TOWN. IT *is* WORTH A STOP TO STROLL THROUGH THE MAIN STREET AND BALDWIN AVENUE SHOPS!

JUST BEYOND PAIA, AT KUAU COVE, IS A RESTAURANT WITH WHAT MAY BE THE MOST BEAUTIFUL VIEW OF MAUI: MAMA'S FISH HOUSE. AND PAST KUAU ON YOUR WAY TO HANA, IS THE VERY SPECTACULAR HO'OKIPA BEACH, FAMED FOR ITS FIFTEEN FOOT WAVES... AND SURFING! HO'OKIPA IS ALWAYS A GOOD AND SOMETIMES THE BEST SURFING BEACH ON MAUI!

MAMA'S FISH HOUSE

STEAK AND SEAFOOD
DINNER NIGHTLY FROM 4:30 PM
RESERVATIONS 579-9612; 579-9248

797 KAIHOLO PLACE
KUAU COVE

THIS RESTAURANT WILL PROBABLY BE
HARD TO FIND EVEN THOUGH IT IS
RIGHT OFF THE HANA HIGHWAY! TAKE
HIGHWAY 36 THROUGH PAIA AND ITS
TINY NEIGHBORING VILLAGE, KUAU.
WATCH FOR THE YELLOW "ANGEL FISH"
SIGN AND TURN LEFT.

STUFFED FISH LANI

MAMA'S FISH HOUSE

2	LBS FISH TRIMMINGS (BONES, HEADS, TAILS FROM WHITE FISH)
1	ONION (SLICED)
1	BUNCH OF PARSLEY
2	CELERY STICKS (DICED)
	JUICE OF ONE LEMON
1	CUP WHITE WINE
1	t SALT
1	CELERY STICK (DICED)
1/2	ONION (DICED)
1	BUNCH PARSLEY (CHOPPED)
2	T CLARIFIED BUTTER
2	CUPS HOMEMADE BROWN BREAD (CUBED)
1	CUP BAY SHRIMP
1	EGG BEATEN
	SALT AND PEPPER (TO TASTE)
	DASH OF CURRY POWDER
4	8-OZ FISH FILETS (MAHIMAHI, ONO, PAKA. ONE INCH THICK.
2	T BUTTER
2	T FLOUR
1	CUP HEAVY CREAM
	SALT AND PEPPER (TO TASTE)
	PINCH OF THYME
1	T BUTTER
1/4	CUP FRESH MUSHROOMS (SLICED)
	CHOPPED PARSLEY (GARNISH)

1. TO MAKE FISH STOCK, PLACE FIRST SEVEN INGREDIENTS IN A LARGE

continued...

STUFFED FISH LANI

(CONTINUED) SAUCE PAN. SIMMER WITH ONE QUART OF WATER FOR 45 MINUTES. SKIM OFF FOAM. STRAIN THROUGH FINE SIEVE (MAKES ABOUT 2 CUPS).

2. TO PREPARE STUFFING SAUTÉ CELERY, ONION AND PARSLEY IN BUTTER IN A MEDIUM SKILLET.

3. ADD BREAD, SHRIMP, EGG, SALT, PEPPER AND CURRY POWDER. MOISTEN WITH FISH STOCK. SET ASIDE AND RESERVE REMAINING FISH STOCK.

4. BUTTERFLY FILETS AND STUFF EACH WITH ABOUT HALF A CUP OF STUFFING. PRESS FIRMLY TOGETHER.

5. BAKE IN 400-DEGREE OVEN FOR 20-25 MINUTES UNTIL FISH IS OPAQUE.

6. TEN MINUTES BEFORE FISH IS BAKED, MAKE A ROUX BY MIXING TOGETHER BUTTER AND FLOUR IN A MEDIUM SAUCE PAN OVER LOW HEAT.

7. SLOWLY ADD ONE CUP OF REMAINING FISH STOCK. BRING TO A BOIL AND COOK 2 MINUTES.

8. ADD CREAM AND SEASONINGS. BEAT WITH A WIRE WISK UNTIL SAUCE COMES TO A BOILING POINT. DO not BOIL!

9. REMOVE FROM HEAT. SET ASIDE. KEEP WARM.

10. WHEN FISH IS BAKED, POUR SAUCE OVER ALL FILETS. GARNISH WITH PARSLEY.

MAMA'S FISH HOUSE

PREPARATION: 25-30 MINUTES
COOKING/ BAKING: ONE HOUR/ 25 MINUTES
SERVES: 4

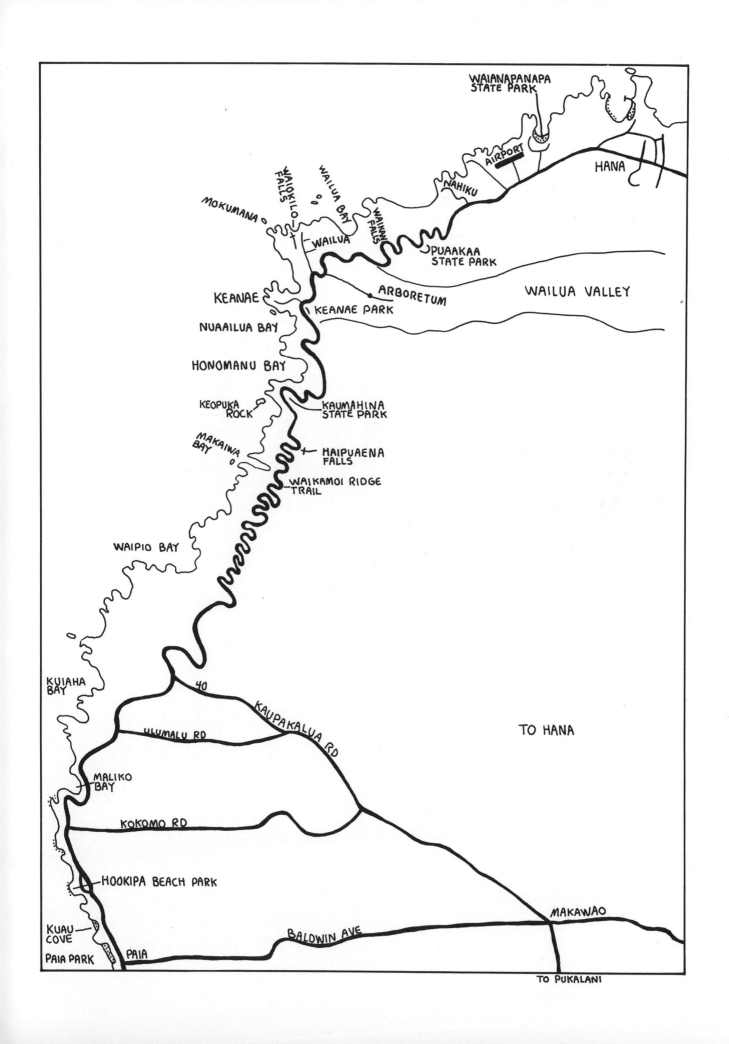

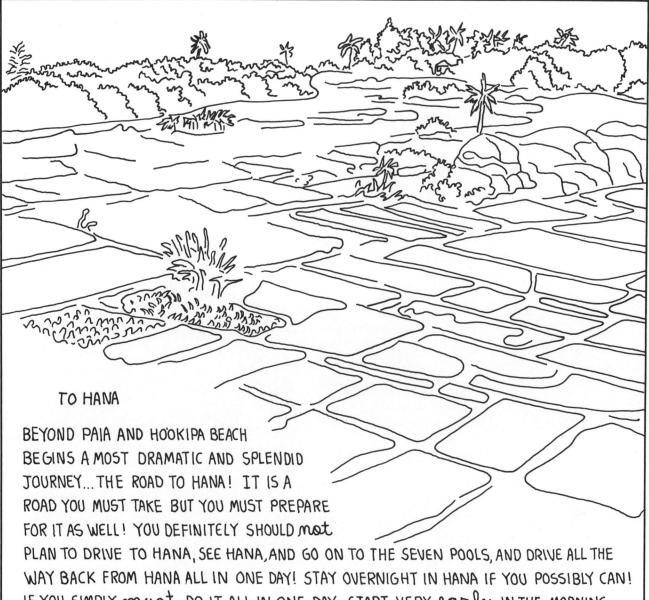

TO HANA

BEYOND PAIA AND HO'OKIPA BEACH
BEGINS A MOST DRAMATIC AND SPLENDID
JOURNEY... THE ROAD TO HANA! IT IS A
ROAD YOU MUST TAKE BUT YOU MUST PREPARE
FOR IT AS WELL! YOU DEFINITELY SHOULD *not*
PLAN TO DRIVE TO HANA, SEE HANA, AND GO ON TO THE SEVEN POOLS, AND DRIVE ALL THE
WAY BACK FROM HANA ALL IN ONE DAY! STAY OVERNIGHT IN HANA IF YOU POSSIBLY CAN!
IF YOU SIMPLY *must* DO IT ALL IN ONE DAY, START VERY *early* IN THE MORNING.
HAVE PICNIC GOODIES WITH YOU AND PLAN TO ENJOY THEM ON THE WAY. DON'T EVEN
TAKE THIS TRIP IF YOU WILL BE RUSHED- YOU WON'T ENJOY IT, YOU WILL BE PLACING YOUR-
SELF IN DANGER OF AN ACCIDENT OR DAMAGE TO YOUR VEHICLE (NO FUN TO BE STRANDED,
EVEN ON MAUI), AND YOU'LL BE MISSING THE WHOLE POINT OF YOUR VISIT, WHICH IS TO SEE
and FEEL MAUI! THE JOURNEY IS EXQUISITE SO YOU'LL WANT TO STOP OFTEN ANYWAY!
THERE ARE OVER 600 CURVES AND BY THE TIME YOU RETURN YOU'LL SWEAR THEY HAVE ADDED
A THOUSAND MORE! THERE ARE 60 BRIDGES, MOST OF WHICH ARE "ONE-WAY"(AND SOMEHOW ALWAYS
THE WRONG WAY!) AND THERE ARE POTHOLES. CHUCKHOLES. CRATERS. TENS OF THOUSANDS
OF THEM, EACH ONE INESCAPABLY IN FRONT OF YOUR POOR TIRES!

BUT IT IS A WONDERFUL DRIVE, ESPECIALLY WHEN YOU HAVE ANTICIPATED AND DISCOUNTED
THE RIGORS ALONG THE WAY AND CAN THUS PAY ATTENTION TO THE WONDERS INSTEAD!

HANA

HANA

HEAVENLY, TROPICAL HANA! WHERE ALOHA IS STILL A REALITY AND CHARM AND HOSPITALITY ARE AS PLENTIFUL AS THE TROPICAL FLOWERS! WITH ONLY A FEW HUNDRED RESIDENTS AND AN ISOLATION PROVIDED DUE TO THE DIFFICULT NATURE OF THE ROADS LEADING TO IT AND THE LACK OF A FUNCTIONING WHARF, HANA IS A DIFFERENT WORLD! A WORLD OF QUIET AND BEAUTY WHICH WILL FORCE YOU TO RELAX AND ENJOY IT!

BECAUSE IT IS SO BEAUTIFUL AND QUIET HANA HAS ALWAYS BEEN PERCEIVED TO HAVE *mana* (SPIRITUAL FORCE). THIS VALLEY ON THE EASTERN FLANK OF HALEAKALA HAS OFTEN BEEN A BATTLEFIELD! FOR EXAMPLE, DURING THE LATE 1770s KAHEKILI OF MAUI AND KALANIOPUU OF HAWAII FOUGHT FIERCE BATTLES HERE. HANA AND MAUI COASTLINES FACING HAWAI'I (THE BIG ISLAND) WERE OFTEN THE PROPERTY OF HAWAI'I, NOT MAUI!

IN 1778 CAPTAIN COOK VISITED HANA ON HIS VOYAGE OF "DISCOVERY" OF THE ISLANDS. BY 1860 THERE WAS A SUGAR PLANTATION WHICH CONTINUED IN OPERATION UNTIL THE GREAT DEPRESSION. THEN THE LATE PAUL FAGAN BOUGHT IT AND CREATED THE HANA RANCH COMPANY, NOW A 15,000 ACRE WORKING-RANCH, AND THE WORLD-CLASS RESORT AND A MAUI LANDMARK: HOTEL HANA MAUI. NOW IT IS THE RICH, THE FAMOUS, THE "STARS" FROM AROUND THE WORLD WHO COME TO THIS QUIET, ISOLATED PLACE OF EXQUISITE BEAUTY, SEEKING SOME TWENTIETH CENTURY FORM OF *mana*! BUT HANA DOESN'T CARE IF YOU ARE "FAMOUS" OR UNKNOWN, AS THE BEAUTY AND ENCHANTMENT ARE FREELY GIVEN TO EVERYONE!

HANA WHARF

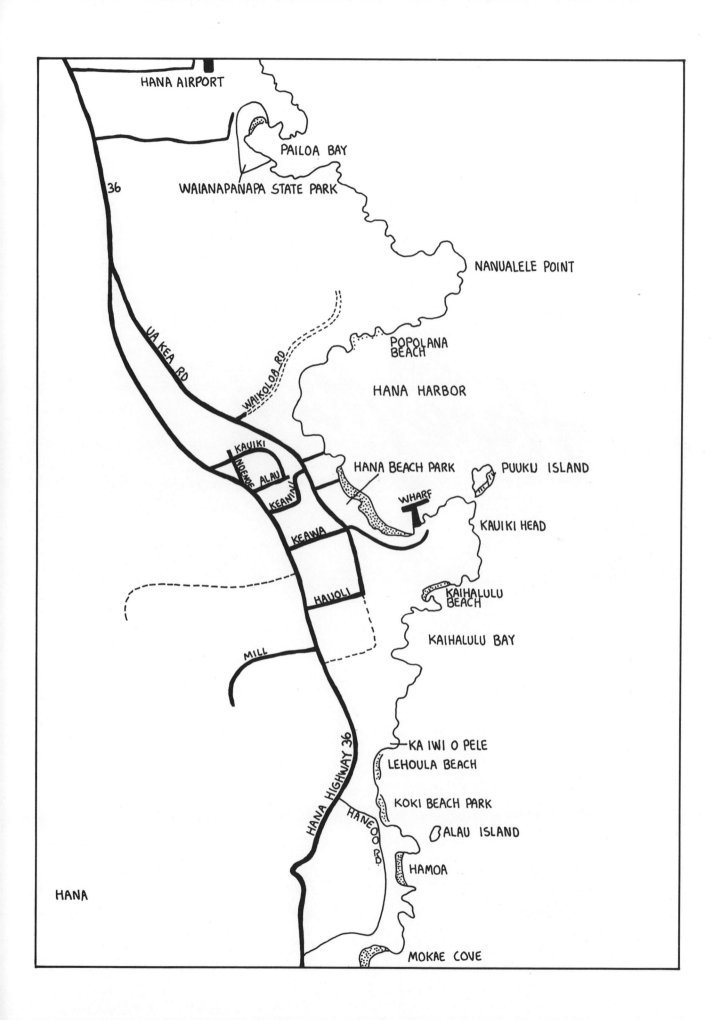

HOTEL

Hana-Maui

HOTEL DINING ROOM

BREAKFAST 7:30-10
BUFFET 12-2
DINNER 6:30-8
AMERICAN CUISINE
248-8211

HANA RANCH RESTAURANT
BUFFET 10-3:30
DINNER 5:30-8
248-8255

HOTEL

Hana-Maui

THE DINING ROOM

SHRIMP SCAMPI CASSEROLE

1/2	LB SPAGHETTI NOODLES	
8	JUMBO PRAWNS	
2	OZ CAPERS	
1/2	CUP WHITE WINE	
1	CUP BUTTER (SOFTENED)	
3	T SHALLOTS	
3	CLOVES GARLIC (MINCED)	
1/2	t WHITE PEPPER	

CONTINUED...

1/4 CUP PARSLEY (CHOPPED)

JUICE OF ONE LEMON

DASH OF LEA & PERRINS WORCESTERSHIRE SAUCE

1. BOIL SPAGHETTI UNTIL AL DENTE. PLACE IN MEDIUM CASSEROLE DISH. SET ASIDE. KEEP WARM.
2. CLEAN, PEEL AND DEVEIN PRAWNS. RESERVE SHELLS.
3. PLACE CLEANED PRAWNS BACK INTO SHELLS. PUT IN SMALL CASSEROLE DISH.
4. PREHEAT OVEN TO 450 DEGREES.
5. IN A SMALL SAUCEPAN, OVER MEDIUM HEAT, BOIL CAPERS AND WINE TOGETHER FOR TEN MINUTES. (REDUCE LIQUID BY ONE-HALF.)
6. MEANWHILE, IN A SMALL MIXING BOWL, MIX TOGETHER BUTTER, SHALLOTS, GARLIC, PEPPER, WORCESTERSHIRE SAUCE, PARSLEY AND LEMON JUICE. SET ASIDE.
7. REMOVE CAPERS AND WINE FROM HEAT; MASH WITH FORK; ADD TO BUTTER MIXTURE.
8. SPOON BUTTER SAUCE OVER TOP OF PRAWNS IN CASSEROLE DISH AND BAKE IN PREHEATED OVEN 7-10 MINUTES.
9. REMOVE FROM OVEN. PLACE PRAWNS ON TOP OF COOKED SPAGHETTI NOODLES.
10. SPOON REMAINING BUTTER SAUCE OVER ALL. PLACE IN OVEN JUST TO MELT BUTTER.

PREPARATION: 20 MINUTES

COOKING/BAKING: 15/ 10-12 MINUTES

SERVES: 4

HOTEL

Hana-Maui

STUFFED MUSHROOMS HANA STYLE

1   CUP COOKED CHICKEN (FINELY CHOPPED)
2   T CURRY POWDER
2   T BRANDY
1   t ACCENT
1   T MAYONNAISE
JUICE FROM 1/2 LIME
SALT (TO TASTE)
24 MUSHROOM CAPS
2   T CRISP BACON (CRUMBLED)
1   HARD BOILED EGG (MINCED)
2   T COCONUT (GRATED)
2   T PARSLEY (CHOPPED)

1. IN A MEDIUM BOWL MIX TOGETHER CHICKEN, CURRY POWDER, BRANDY, ACCENT, MAYONNAISE LIME JUICE AND SALT.
2. PRESS ONE TEASPOON OF MIXTURE INTO EACH MUSHROOM CAP.
3. SPRINKLE BACON, EGG, COCONUT AND PARSLEY OVER TOP
4. BAKE IN 400 DEGREE OVEN FOR 20 MINUTES.
5. SERVE HOTEL HANA MAUI'S FAMOUS STUFFED MUSHROOMS IN YOUR OWN HOME...AND ENJOY!

PREPARATION: 10 MINUTES
BAKING: 20 MINUTES
SERVES: 8-12

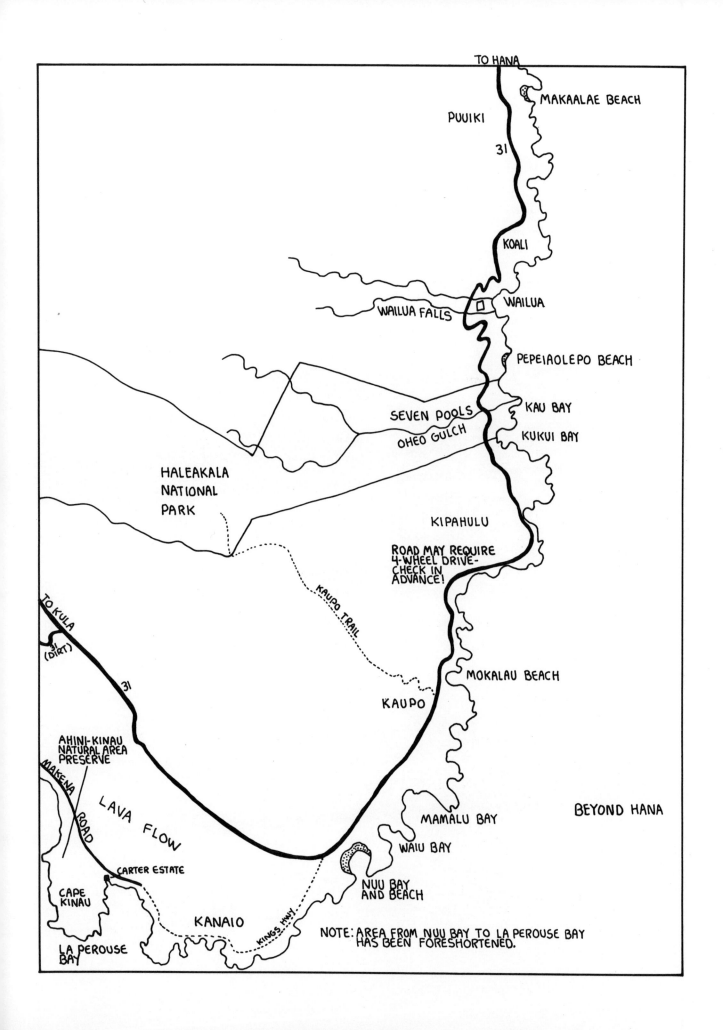

TO HANA

MAKAALAE BEACH

PUUIKI

31

KOALI

WAILUA FALLS

WAILUA

PEPEIAOLEPO BEACH

SEVEN POOLS

KAU BAY

OHEO GULCH

KUKUI BAY

HALEAKALA
NATIONAL
PARK

KIPAHULU

ROAD MAY REQUIRE
4-WHEEL DRIVE-
CHECK IN
ADVANCE!

TO KULA

31 (DIRT)

KAUPO TRAIL

31

MOKALAU BEACH

KAUPO

AHINI-KINAU
NATURAL AREA
PRESERVE

MAKENA ROAD

LAVA FLOW

BEYOND HANA

MAMALU BAY

WAIU BAY

CARTER ESTATE

CAPE
KINAU

NUU BAY
AND BEACH

KANAIO

KINGS HWY

LA PEROUSE
BAY

NOTE: AREA FROM NUU BAY TO LA PEROUSE BAY
HAS BEEN FORESHORTENED.

KIPAHULU

BEYOND HANA

TAKE THE PI'ILANI HIGHWAY, 31, SOUTH PAST HANA. IF YOU
HAVE A STURDY VEHICLE AND IF THERE HAS BEEN NO RECENT
ROAD DAMAGE (CHECK BEFOREHAND) YOU MAY DECIDE NOT
TO RETURN VIA THE HANA HIGHWAY BUT INSTEAD MAY
CHOOSE TO DRIVE BEHIND HALEAKALA TO KULA
(31 BECOMES 37) OR TO DRIVE TO WAILEA
(31 BECOMES A SHORT GRAVEL ROAD WHICH
TAKES YOU DOWN-SLOPE TO MAKENA AND
THEN ON TO WAILEA.)

A FEW MILES PAST HANA IS A RED CINDER
HILL NAMED KA IWI O PELE (THE BONES
OF PELE). ON THE RIGHT OF THE HILL
IS KOKI BEACH PARK WHOSE BEACH
IS LOVELY BUT UNSAFE. PAST KOKI
AT MOKAE COVE IS A THOUSAND
FOOT BEACH THAT WAS FAMOUS EVEN
IN ANCIENT TIMES FOR SURFING AND
SWIMMING! A BEACH IN THE NORTH PACIFIC
WHICH JAMES MICHENER SAYS LOOKS MORE LIKE
A SOUTH PACIFIC BEACH THAN ANY SOUTH PACIFIC BEACH:
HAMOA BEACH! ACCESS IS HANA RANCH PROPERTY.

MGM USED THE WAILUA AREA FOR FILMING "MUTINY
ON THE BOUNTY." TWO STREAMS AND THUS TWO WATER-
FALLS RUSH OUT OF THE VALLEY!
KIPAHULU, THE PARK DISTRICT ON
THE SOUTH SIDE OF HALEAKALA,
INCLUDES THE FABLED SEVEN
POOLS PARK (OHEO GULCH).
SWIMMING PERMITTED-AND IN THE
VERY POOLS WHERE MAUI'S MOM
ONCE WASHED HER TAPA CLOTH! FARTHER
ALONG IS LINDBERG'S GRAVE. FROM KAUPO
ON AROUND THE ISLAND TO MAKENA, IS A RUGGED
COASTAL REGION, A PARADISE FOR HIKERS AND FISHERMEN!

KAUPO

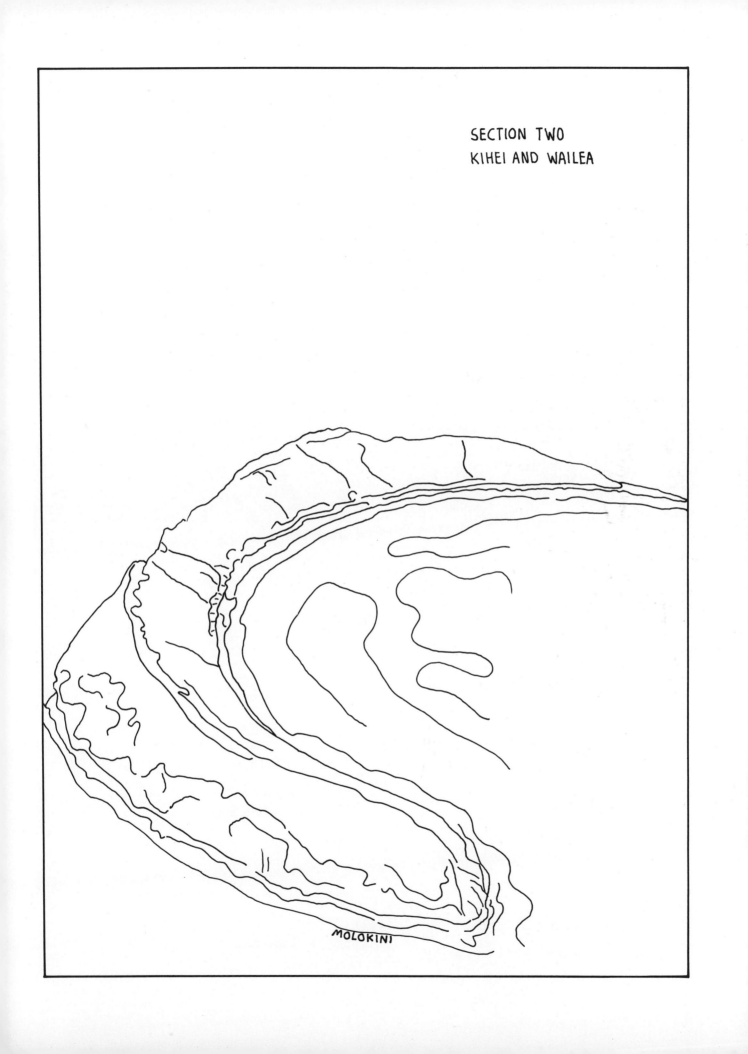

MOLOKINI

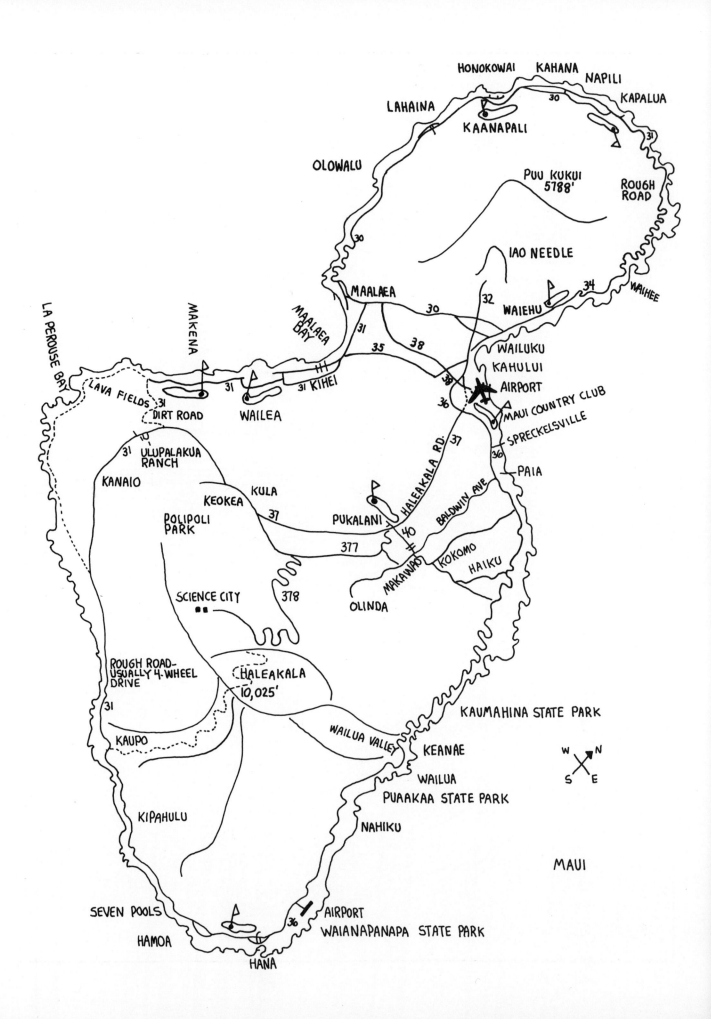

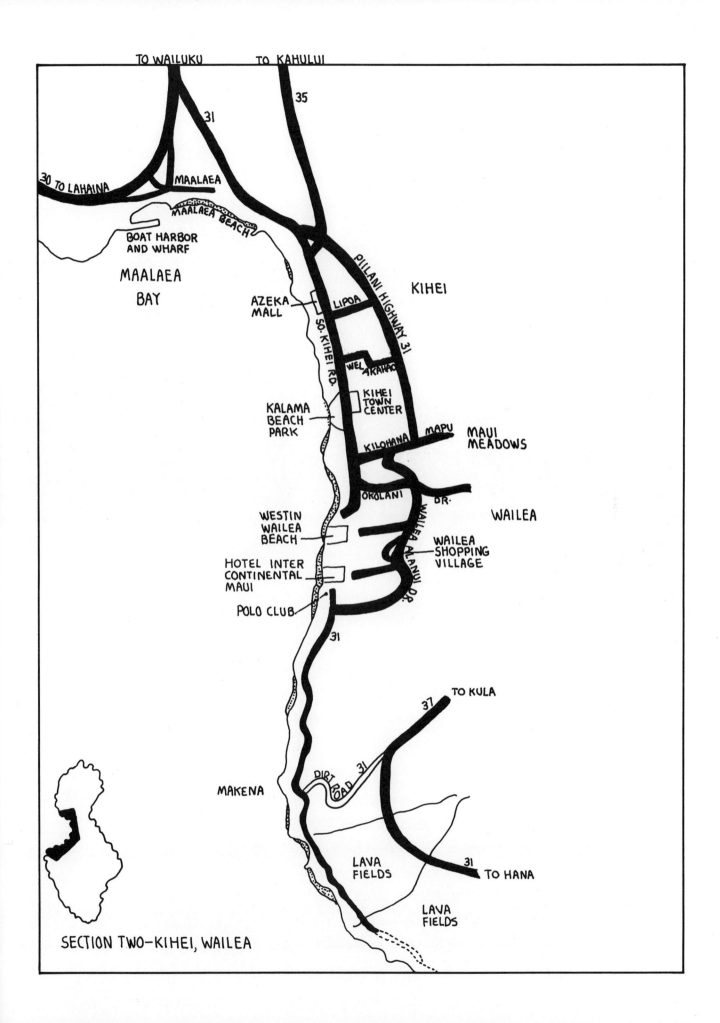

SECTION TWO—KIHEI, WAILEA

SECTION TWO

MAALAEA. KIHEI. WAILEA.

THIS SECTION RESTS NEXT TO THE OCEAN ON THE LEEWARD SLOPES OF HALEAKALA, FROM MAALAEA BAY TO MAKENA. HERE YOU WILL FIND TWO WORLD-CLASS RESORTS, THE WESTIN WAILEA BEACH AND THE INTER CONTINENTAL MAUI, TWO 18-HOLE GOLF COURSES, THE FINEST TENNIS FACILITIES ON MAUI, EXCELLENT WHITE SAND BEACHES, WONDERFUL DIVING, SNORKELING, SWIMMING AND SURFING. WE RECOMMEND SIX RESTAURANTS IN SECTION TWO: WATERFRONT RESTAURANT AT MAALAEA; ROBAIRE'S IN KIHEI; RAFFLES AND PALM COURT IN THE WESTIN; AMBROSIA RESTAURANTE IN THE WAILEA SHOPPING VILLAGE; AND LA PEROUSE IN THE INTER CONTINENTAL.

MAALAEA BAY HAS A THREE-MILE WHITE SAND SHORELINE WITH GOOD SURFING NEAR THE BOAT HARBOR. THE HARBOR WAS BUILT IN 1952 FOR RECREATIONAL PURPOSES. SWIMMING IS GENERALLY SAFE ON THIS UNDEVELOPED BEACH, WHICH IS POPULAR WITH LOCALS (WHO ARE RESIGNED TO THE EVER-BLOWING AFTERNOON WINDS)!

KIHEI IS SAID TO BE THE SPOT WHERE VANCOUVER ALIGHTED IN THE 1800'S. THE HAWAIIAN WORD "KIHEI" MEANS "SHAWL", LIKELY THE RECTANGULAR "TAPA" (QUILT MADE FROM BARK) CLOAK WHICH WAS TIED IN A KNOT ON ONE SHOULDER. NOW "KIHEI" MEANS SHORELINE RESORTS AND CONDOMINIUMS! KIHEI (KALEPOLEPO BEACH) WAS ONCE (IN THE NINETEENTH CENTURY) A VILLAGE VISITED BY HAWAIIAN NOBILITY. KIHEI IN ITS MODERN

ASPECT IS THE PRODUCT OF THE TREMENDOUS BUILDING BOOM OF THE 1970'S, WHICH TURNED THIS STRIP OF MAUI INTO A RESORT AREA. WITH SO MANY COMPETITIVE DEVELOPMENT INTERESTS INVOLVED IT WAS INEVITABLE, PERHAPS, THAT KIHEI WOULD NOT HAVE THE PLANNED CHARM OF THE OTHER RESORT AREAS. BUT THE AREA IS VERY POPULAR, WITH MANY FINE FACILITIES AND PLEASANT, SAFE BEACHES. THERE IS ALSO MUCH SUNSHINE, AS THE RAIN CLOUDS FROM HALEAKALA RARELY WANDER AS FAR NORTH AS KIHEI! IN THE SLEEPY, WAR-DOMINATED YEARS OF THE 1940'S, WHEN "KAANAPALI" MEANT SUGAR CANE AND "WAILEA" WAS BUT A ROCKY POINT ON A BEACH, AN *acre* OF KIHEI BEACHFRONT SOLD FOR UNDER $1000! YOU MIGHT BE ABLE TO BUY A BEACHFRONT *lot* FOR A MILLION DOLLARS TODAY!

WAILEA IS A PLANNED RESORT OF 1450 ACRES SOUTH OF KIHEI, WHICH IS MORE CONVENIENTLY APPROACHED BY THE PIILANI HIGHWAY, 31, RATHER THAN THE CLUTTERED SOUTH KIHEI ROAD. WAILEA FRONTS ON MILES OF EXCELLENT WHITE SAND BEACHES. THE BEACHES ARE, IN SEQUENCE FROM KIHEI: KEAWAKAPU, MOKAPU, ULUA, WAILEA AND POLO. THIS PLANNED COMMUNITY WAS DEVELOPED BY ALEXANDER & BALDWIN (OWNER OF HC&S- HAWAIIAN-COMMERCIAL & SUGAR- MAUI'S LARGEST EMPLOYER) IN THE NINETEEN-SEVENTIES. WAILEA IS A BEAUTIFUL RESORT, WORLD- CLASS IN EVERY RESPECT. IT CONSISTS OF TWO ELEGANT HOTEL-COMPLEXES, THE WESTIN WAILEA BEACH AND THE INTER CONTINENTAL MAUI, BEAUTIFUL CONDOMINIUMS AND PRIVATE RESIDENCES, A TOWN SHOPPING VILLAGE, RESTAURANTS AND SHOPS, GOLF AND TENNIS, DIVING, SNORKELING, SAILING, DEEP- SEA FISHING AND SWIMMING!

SOUTH, BEYOND WAILEA, THERE ARE EXCELLENT UNDEVELOPED BEACHES, VERY POPULAR WITH LOCALS. MAKENA WAS ONCE A BUSY TOWN IN-VOLVED IN SUGAR AND CATTLE TRADE FROM UP-SLOPE. SEIBU, A CONSORTIUM OF JAPANESE DEVELOPERS, HAS PLANS TO TURN MAKENA INTO A RESORT. ALONG THE COAST TOWARDS HANA THE SHORES ARE RUGGED, GENERALLY UNPROTECTED FROM THE OCEAN AND DANGEROUS. THIS IS A WONDERFULLY WILD AND CHALLENGING AREA, ONLY FOR THE HARDY AND ADVENTUROUS!

SEAFOOD AND STEAK

DINNER 5:30
LOCATED IN THE MILOWAI CONDOMINIUMS
HAUOLI STREET
MAALAEA
244-9028

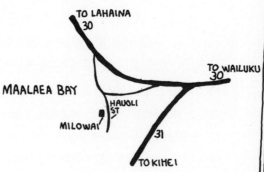

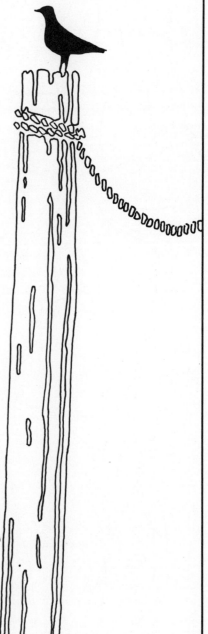

POACHED FISH WITH DILL SAUCE

2	T BUTTER
2	T SHALLOTS (FINELY DICED)
1|2	CUP WHITE WINE
1	t LEMON JUICE
2	SIX-OUNCE FISH FILETS
1	T FLOUR
1	T BUTTER
1|2	CUP FISH STOCK (SEE RECIPE ON NEXT PAGE)
1	t DILL WEED (CHOPPED)

SALT AND PEPPER TO TASTE
1|4   CUP HEAVY CREAM
FRESH CHOPPED DILL (GARNISH)

THE WATERFRONT

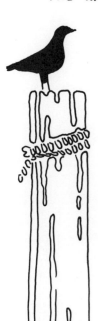

1. IN A LARGE SKILLET WITH MELTED BUTTER SAUTÉ SHALLOTS UNTIL TRANSPARENT. DO NOT BROWN.
2. ADD WINE, LEMON JUICE AND ONE-FOURTH CUP WATER. ADD FILETS AND POACH OVER LOW HEAT UNTIL FISH FLAKES (7-10 MINUTES).
3. REMOVE FILETS FROM SKILLET. PLACE ON A SERVING PLATTER.
4. MAKE A ROUX BY MIXING TOGETHER FLOUR AND BUTTER. SLOWLY ADD TO SKILLET. COOK ONE MINUTE.
5. ADD FISH STOCK AND REDUCE VOLUME TO ABOUT ONE-HALF. SAUCE SHOULD BE THICK.
6. ADD SEASONINGS AND CREAM. COOK 2-3 MINUTES LONGER.
7. POUR SAUCE OVER FILETS AND GARNISH WITH FRESH, CHOPPED DILL.

PREPARATION: 5 MINUTES
COOKING: 20-25 MINUTES
SERVES: 2

NEW ENGLAND STYLE FISH CHOWDER

1   ONION (DICED)
4   STALKS OF CELERY (DICED)
4   STRIPS OF BACON (DICED)
1/2 CUP CLARIFIED BUTTER
1/2 CUP FLOUR
1   *QUART FISH STOCK (RECIPE BELOW)
1   PINT MILK
3   MEDIUM POTATOES (DICED)
1-1/2 LB FRESH WHITEFISH (DICED)
PINCH OF THYME
DASH OF WORCESTERSHIRE SAUCE
SALT AND PEPPER (TO TASTE)
2   BAY LEAVES
2   SPRIGS PARSLEY (CHOPPED)

THE WATERFRONT

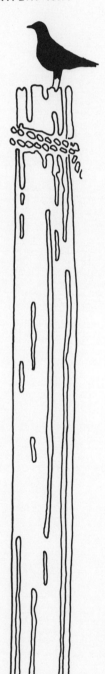

1. IN A MEDIUM SAUCEPAN, WITH MELTED BUTTER, SAUTÉ ONIONS, CELERY AND BACON.
2. ADD FLOUR. COOK 2-3 MINUTES. DO NOT BROWN.
3. ADD HOT FISH STOCK AND MILK. BRING TO A GENTLE BOIL.
4. IN A SEPARATE PAN, BLANCH POTATOES, DRAIN AND ADD TO SOUP. (10-15 MINUTES)
5. ADD FISH AND REMAINING SEASONINGS. BRING TO A GENTLE BOIL AND SIMMER FOR 15 MINUTES.

PREPARATION: 20-25 MINUTES
COOKING: 40-45 MINUTES
YIELD: 2 QUARTS

*FISH STOCK: COVER 2 LBS WHITE FISH BONES WITH ONE QUART WATER. ADD PARSLEY, PINCH OF THYME, 2 BAY LEAVES, SALT AND PEPPER. BRING TO GENTLE BOIL. SIMMER 20 MINUTES. SKIM AS IT BOILS. STRAIN.

MAALAEA

THE OLD HOME OF THE WHALING FLEET, MAALAEA IS NOW THE HOME OF THE MAUI FISHING FLEET AND THE COAST GUARD. MANY OCEAN ACTIVITIES ORIGINATE FROM THIS HARBOR, ESPECIALLY THOSE HEADING FOR MOLOKINI, THE VOLCANIC CRATER VISIBLE BETWEEN KAHOOLAWE AND MAUI. MOLOKINI HAS SOME OF THE BEST DIVING AND SNORKELING WATERS IN HAWAII.

EWA HAVE DONE SOME DAMAGE, WHICH IS BEING ...

KIHEI (KALEPOLEPO BEACH) WAS A BUSY LITTLE VILLAGE IN THE MID-NINETEENTH CENTURY, BEING VISITED BOTH BY HAWAIIAN ALII (NOBILITY) AND WHALING CREWS FROM MAALAEA BAY. A CAPTAIN HALSTEAD BUILT HIS "KOA HOUSE" HERE AND IT REMAINED A TRADING CENTER UNTIL WHALERS NO LONGER CALLED (1870).

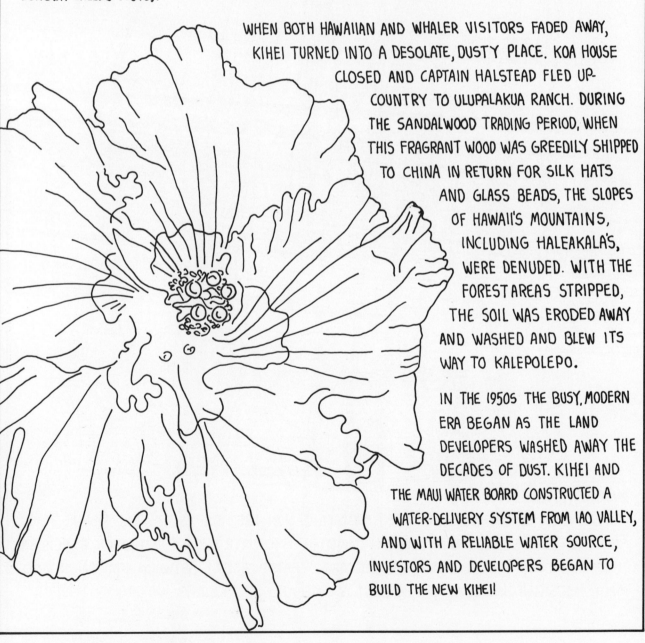

WHEN BOTH HAWAIIAN AND WHALER VISITORS FADED AWAY, KIHEI TURNED INTO A DESOLATE, DUSTY PLACE. KOA HOUSE CLOSED AND CAPTAIN HALSTEAD FLED UP-COUNTRY TO ULUPALAKUA RANCH. DURING THE SANDALWOOD TRADING PERIOD, WHEN THIS FRAGRANT WOOD WAS GREEDILY SHIPPED TO CHINA IN RETURN FOR SILK HATS AND GLASS BEADS, THE SLOPES OF HAWAII'S MOUNTAINS, INCLUDING HALEAKALA'S, WERE DENUDED. WITH THE FOREST AREAS STRIPPED, THE SOIL WAS ERODED AWAY AND WASHED AND BLEW ITS WAY TO KALEPOLEPO.

IN THE 1950s THE BUSY, MODERN ERA BEGAN AS THE LAND DEVELOPERS WASHED AWAY THE DECADES OF DUST. KIHEI AND THE MAUI WATER BOARD CONSTRUCTED A WATER-DELIVERY SYSTEM FROM IAO VALLEY, AND WITH A RELIABLE WATER SOURCE, INVESTORS AND DEVELOPERS BEGAN TO BUILD THE NEW KIHEI!

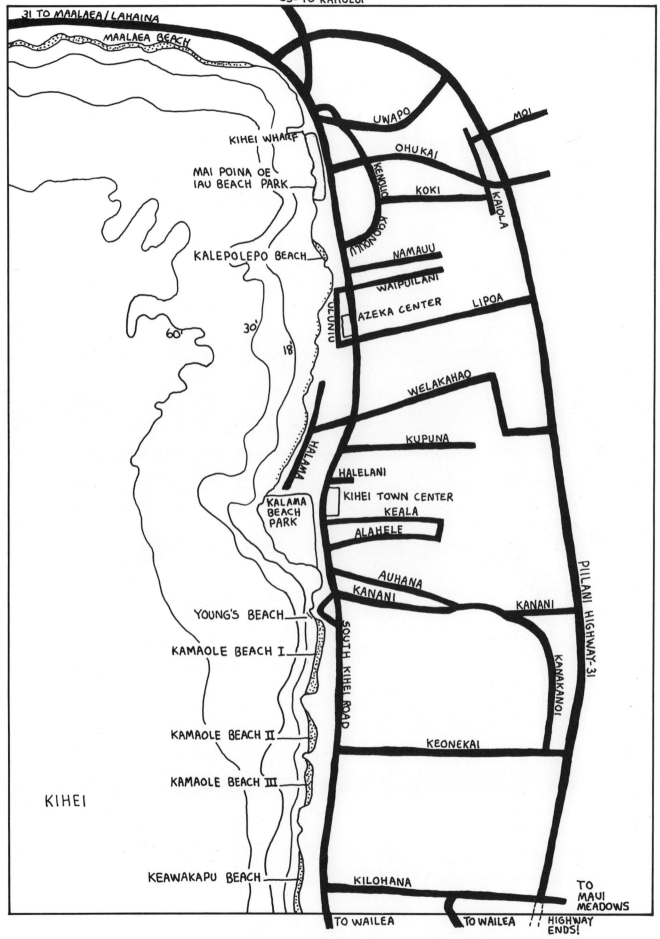

35- TO KAHULUI

31 TO MAALAEA/LAHAINA

MAALAEA BEACH

KIHEI WHARF

UWAPO

MOI

OHUKAI

MAI POINA OE
IAU BEACH PARK

KENOLIO

KOKI

KAIOLA

KONONLU

NAMAUU

KALEPOLEPO BEACH

WAIPUILANI

LIPOA

AZEKA CENTER

OLUNIO

60'

30'

18

WELAKAHAO

KUPUNA

HALAMA

HALELANI

KALAMA
BEACH
PARK

KIHEI TOWN CENTER

KEALA

ALAHELE

AUHANA

KANANI

KANANI

YOUNG'S BEACH

PIILANI HIGHWAY-31

KAMAOLE BEACH I

SOUTH KIHEI ROAD

KANAKANOI

KAMAOLE BEACH II

KEONEKAI

KAMAOLE BEACH III

KIHEI

KEAWAKAPU BEACH

KILOHANA

TO
MAUI
MEADOWS

TO WAILEA

TO WAILEA

HIGHWAY
ENDS!

FRENCH CUISINE
DINNER 6-10
TUESDAY-SATURDAY
RESERVATIONS
879-2707

61 SO. KIHEI ROAD
KIHEI

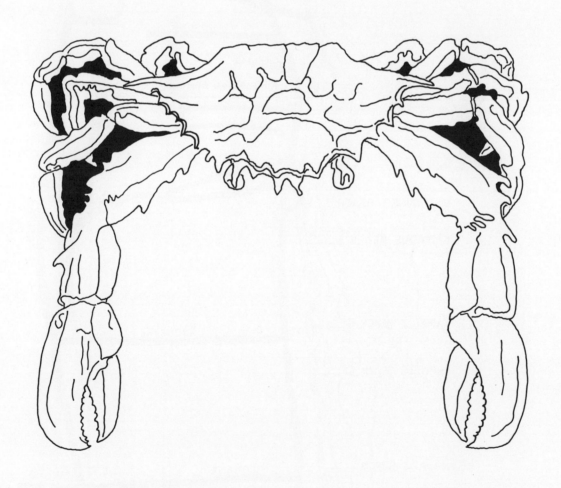

DUCKLING L' ORANGE

FOUR POUND DUCK
SALT AND PEPPER (TO SEASON)

SAUCE L' ORANGE

1/2	CUP SUGAR
1/2	CUP ORANGE JUICE
1/2	CUP VINEGAR
2	CUPS BEEF BROTH
1/2	CUP BUTTER (MELTED)
1/2	CUP FLOUR

1. SEASON DUCK WITH SALT AND PEPPER.
2. ROAST IN 375 DEGREE OVEN FOR ONE AND ONE-HALF TO TWO HOURS (OR UNTIL DONE). MEANWHILE, PREPARE SAUCE L'ORANGE AS FOLLOWS:

SAUCE L' ORANGE

1. IN A SMALL SAUCE PAN MIX TOGETHER SUGAR AND ORANGE JUICE. Continued

2. (CONTINUED) PLACE OVER MEDIUM HEAT AND REDUCE UNTIL MIXTURE TURNS GOLDEN BROWN.
3. ADD VINEGAR AND BOIL FOUR MINUTES LONGER.
4. ADD BEEF BROTH AND COOK FIVE MINUTES MORE.
5. MAKE A ROUX, MIXING TOGETHER THE BUTTER AND FLOUR IN A SECOND SAUCEPAN.
6. SLOWLY ADD ROUX INTO THE ORANGE JUICE MIXTURE UNTIL DESIRED CONSISTANCY (LIKE THIN MAYONNAISE). ALL OF THE ROUX MAY NOT BE NEEDED. SET ASIDE THIS SAUCE L' ORANGE AND KEEP WARM.

7. WHEN DUCK IS FULLY COOKED REMOVE FROM OVEN AND SPLIT LENGTHWISE.
8. PLACE DUCK ON SERVING PLATTER AND POUR SAUCE L' ORANGE OVER TOP.
9. GARNISH WITH ORANGE SLICES.
10. SERVE WITH RICE PILAF AND FRESH VEGETABLES.

PREPARATION: 5 MINUTES
ROASTING/ COOKING: 2 HOURS/ 15-20 MINUTES
SERVES: 4-6

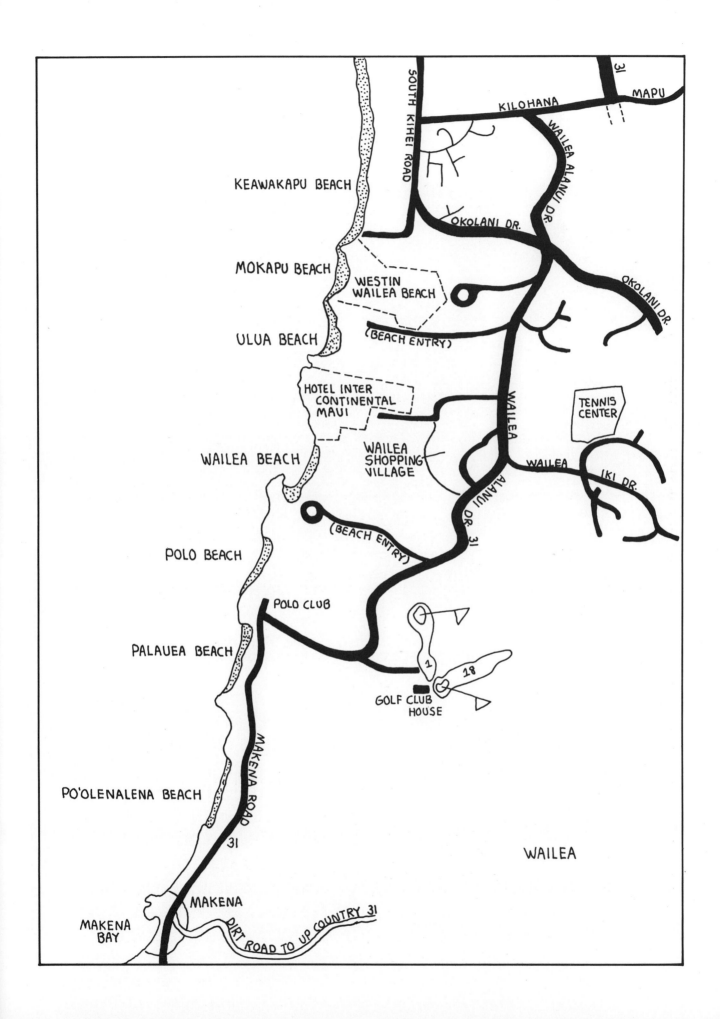

WAILEA IS A 1450 ACRE, SELF-CONTAINED LUXURY RESORT AND
RESIDENTIAL COMPLEX. WITHIN WAILEA ARE TWO WORLD-CLASS HOTEL RESORTS, THE WESTIN
WAILEA BEACH AND THE INTER CONTINENTAL MAUI. TWO DISTINCTIVE 18-HOLE CHAMPIONSHIP
GOLF COURSES ROLL ALONG BETWEEN THE OCEAN AND HALEAKALA VOLCANO. THE TENNIS
CENTER HAS 14 COURTS AND A 1500 SEAT STADIUM. THE HOTELS AND WAILEA SHOPPING VILLAGE
(40,000 SQUARE FEET BUILT AROUND A VILLAGE GREEN) OFFER MANY DISTINCTIVE SHOPS.
WE HAVE CHOSEN FOUR WAILEA RESTAURANTS. FOR YOU: RAFFLES' AND PALM COURT IN THE WESTIN;
AMBROSIA, IN THE WAILEA SHOPPING VILLAGE; AND LA PEROUSE IN THE INTER CONTINENTAL.
WAILEA'S FIVE BEACHES ARE POPULAR WITH VISITORS AND LOCALS. SNORKELING AND SCUBA ARE
AT THEIR BEST IN THESE WATERS. ALSO POPULAR: TRIPS TO MOLOKINI, THE MARINE SANCTUARY.

Raffles'

DINNER SERVED NIGHTLY
6:30-10:30 PM

SUNDAY CHAMPAIGNE BRUNCH
9 AM-2 PM

LOCATED IN THE WESTIN
WAILEA BEACH HOTEL
3550 WAILEA ALANUI DR.
WAILEA

RESERVATIONS
879-4900

SAUTEED ONO CASIMIR

CURRY SAUCE

3	OZ	BUTTER
3	OZ	FLOUR
2	CUPS	FISH STOCK (CAN SUBSTITUTE CHICKEN STOCK)
1	t	CURRY POWDER
2	t	CHUTNEY
1/2	CUP	CREAM

FISH

2	LBS	ONO (SUB: WHITEFISH, SWORDFISH)
4	OZ	BUTTER, CLARIFIED
		BROWN SUGAR (TO COAT)
2		BANANAS (SLICED)

1. IN A SMALL SAUCEPAN MAKE A ROUX, MIXING FLOUR IN MELTED BUTTER (LOW HEAT).
2. ADD FISH STOCK, CURRY POWDER AND BRING MIXTURE TO A BOIL, STIRRING CONSTANTLY.
3. ADD CHUTNEY AND SLOWLY POUR IN THE CREAM. SET ASIDE. KEEP WARM.

1. IN A HEAVY IRON SKILLET PAN-FRY FISH IN MELTED BUTTER UNTIL DONE.
2. REMOVE FISH FROM SKILLET AND PLACE ON SERVING PLATTER. KEEP WARM.
3. COAT BANANAS WITH BROWN SUGAR.
4. IN A SMALL SKILLET FRY BANANAS 2-3 MINUTES.
5. PLACE BANANAS ON TOP OF FISH AND POUR CURRY SAUCE OVER TOP. SERVE WITH RICE.

PREPARATION: 2-3 MINUTES
COOKING: 15-20 MINUTES
SERVES: 4-6

OPAKAPAKA IN SORREL SAUCE

2   LBS OPAKAPAKA FISH* (DEBONED, CUT INTO 4 FILETS)
4   OZ BUTTER
1/2 CUP CREAM
SALT AND PEPPER (TO TASTE)
1   PINCH SORREL (CHEF SINT-NICOLAAS RECOMMENDS FRESH
                   SORREL JULIENNE)

1. PRE-HEAT OVEN AT 375°.
2. BUTTER FILETS AND PLACE THEM IN A BAKING DISH.
3. BAKE 12-15 MINUTES UNTIL DONE.
4. REMOVE FROM OVEN. POUR EXCESS LIQUID INTO A SMALL SAUCEPAN.
5. ADD CREAM AND BRING TO A BOIL.
6. POUR SAUCE OVER TOP OF FISH.
7. SEASON WITH SALT, PEPPER AND SORREL.
8. SERVE WITH FRESH VEGETABLE AND NEW POTATOES.

PREPARATION: 2-3 MINUTES
BAKING / COOKING: 12-15 MINUTES / 5 MINUTES
SERVES: 4

*CAN SUBSTITUTE SNAPPER

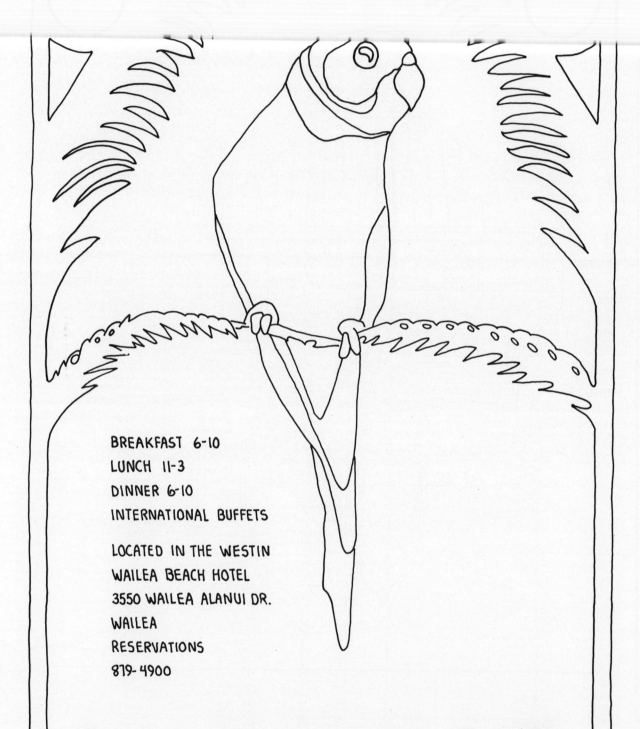

BREAKFAST 6-10
LUNCH 11-3
DINNER 6-10
INTERNATIONAL BUFFETS

LOCATED IN THE WESTIN
WAILEA BEACH HOTEL
3550 WAILEA ALANUI DR.
WAILEA
RESERVATIONS
879- 4900

PALM COURT

PALM COURT

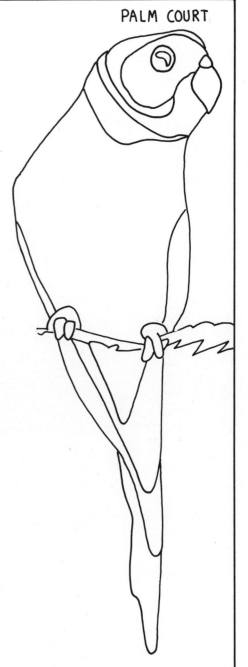

CURRIED CHICKEN AND PAPAYA

1   5 LB. CHICKEN
3   PAPAYAS (CUT INTO 6 HALVES)
1   CUP MAYONNAISE
1-1/2 CUP YOGHURT OR SOUR CREAM
2   T CURRY POWDER
2   T CHUTNEY
COCONUT FLAKES (GARNISH)

1.   COOK, DEBONE AND SHRED CHICKEN.
2.   REMOVE SEEDS FROM PAPAYAS AND PLACE
     PAPAYA HALVES ON A SERVING DISH.
3.   MIX TOGETHER MAYONNAISE, YOGHURT, CURRY
     POWDER AND CHUTNEY. MIX WITH CHICKEN.
4.   PLACE ONE-SIXTH OF CHICKEN MIXTURE INTO
     SEED CAVITY OF EACH PAPAYA HALF.
5.   SPRINKLE WITH COCONUT.

PREPARATION: 5 MINUTES
COOKING: 2 HOURS (THIS CAN BE DONE AHEAD OF
                  TIME AND THE CHICKEN PLACED
                  IN REFRIGERATOR UNTIL READY TO USE.)
SERVES: 6

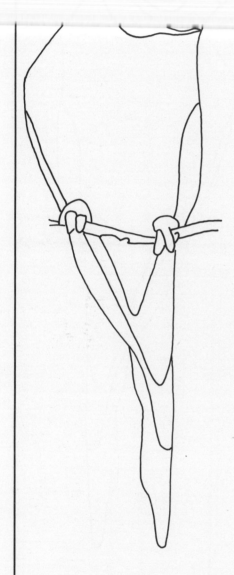

MAUI ONION RINGS

2   MAUI ONIONS* (SLICED 1/4 INCH THIN
     AND SEPARATED INTO RINGS)
1   CUP PANCAKE MIX
1   CUP PANKO BREADING
OIL FOR DEEP FRYING

1. MAKE A BATTER BY ADDING 3/4 CUP WATER
   TO PANCAKE MIX.
2. COVER ONIONS WITH PANCAKE BATTER.
3. COAT ONIONS WITH BREADING.
4. DEEP FRY ONION RINGS IN HOT OIL
   UNTIL GOLDEN BROWN.
5. SERVE IMMEDIATELY WITH YOUR FAVORITE
   HAMBURGER.

PREPARATION: 15 MINUTES
COOKING: 3-5 MINUTES
SERVES: 4
*THESE ARE FAMOUS ONION RINGS IN MAUI BECAUSE
OF THE DELICIOUS MAUI ONION! SUBSTITUTE A GOOD
SWEET ONION.

LA PEROUSE

"AFTER HAVING STEERED SOUTHWEST BY WEST, AS FAR AS THE SOUTHWEST POINT OF THE ISLAND OF MOWEE, I HAULED TO THE WEST AND AFTERWARDS TO THE NORTHWEST IN ORDER TO GAIN ANCHORAGE...THE INLIANS (!) OF THE VILLAGES, HASTENED ALONGSIDE IN THEIR CANOES, BRINGING AS ARTICLES OF BARTER HOGS, SWEET POTATOES, BANANAS..." SO WROTE CAPTAIN LA PEROUSE IN THE SHIPS LOGBOOK DESCRIBING HIS ARRIVAL HERE ON THE 30TH OF MAY 1786.

LA PEROUSE, DESCRIBED AS ONE OF THE GREAT NAVIGATORS OF THE 18TH CENTURY, STAYED HERE FOR ONLY A SHORT WHILE, DEPARTING WITH FRESH PROVISIONS...FRESH AS ONLY THIS LUSH TROPICAL CLIME AND THE PACIFIC OCEAN CAN PRODUCE.

THE HOTEL INTER-CONTINENTAL MAUI IS SITUATED CLOSE TO THE BEAUTIFUL LA PEROUSE BAY.

INTERNATIONAL CUISINE
DINNER NIGHTLY 6:30-11:00
RESERVATIONS
879-1922

LA PEROUSE

FROGLEGS PROVENCALE

10   SINGLE FROGLEGS (SMALL SIZE)
SALT (TO TASTE)
WHITE PEPPER (TO TASTE)
FLOUR (TO DREDGE)
EGG WASH (1 EGG MIXED WITH 1 t WATER)
3   OZ BUTTER
1|2 t GARLIC (FINELY CHOPPED)
1|2 CUP TOMATO CONCASSEE
1|2 t PARSLEY (FINELY CHOPPED)

1. SPLIT FROGLEGS IN HALF. REMOVE FEET.
2. SEASON WITH SALT AND PEPPER. DREDGE IN FLOUR. SHAKE OFF ALL EXCESS FLOUR.
3. PLACE IN EGG WASH. REMOVE.
4. IN A SMALL SKILLET, IN 3T. CLARIFIED BUTTER, SAUTÉ FROGLEGS UNTIL GOLDEN BROWN.
5. REMOVE FROM PAN. DISCARD BUTTER.
6. ADD REMAINING BUTTER TO PAN AND SAUTÉ GARLIC.
7. PUT FROGLEGS BACK IN PAN; ADD TOMATO AND PARSLEY. SEASON. COOK 2-3 MINUTES.
8. SERVE WITH RICE PILAF AND BROCCOLI HOLLANDAISE.

PREPARATION: 15-20 MINUTES
COOKING: 5-10 MINUTES
SERVES: 2

SOUP DE FRAISE

1	CUP JULIENNE OF ORANGE ZEST (PEEL USED AS A FLAVORING)
4	OZ SUGAR
1/2	CUP GRENADINE
1/2	CUP WHISKEY
1	CUP STRAWBERRIES
1/2	CUP BLUEBERRIES
1/2	CUP BLACKBERRIES
1	CUP RASPBERRIES
2	BOTTLES BEAUJOLAIS WINE
2	CUPS FRESH ORANGE JUICE
1	CUP FRESH LEMON JUICE
24	OZ STRAWBERRY SHERBET

CRUSHED BLACK PEPPER

1. IN A MEDIUM SAUCEPAN COOK ZEST, SUGAR AND GRENADINE TOGETHER. WHEN ALMOST CARMELIZED, FLAME WITH WHISKEY.
2. ADD HALF OF THE FRUITS, PERHAPS A LITTLE MORE SUGAR AND COOK 2-4 MIN.
3. ADD WINE AND FRUIT JUICES, BRING TO BOIL. SIMMER 20 MINUTES AND SEASON WITH PEPPER.
4. PUT LIQUID AND FRUIT THROUGH FOOD MILL AND COMBINE WITH THE OTHER HALF OF THE FRUITS. CHILL THOROUGHLY.
5. IN A LARGE RED WINE GLASS PUT 4 OZ. OF FRUIT MIXTURE. ON TOP, PLACE 4 OZ. STRAWBERRY SHERBET.

PREPARATION: 5 MINUTES
COOKING: 40 MINUTES
SERVES: 6

HOTEL INTER CONTINENTAL MAUI

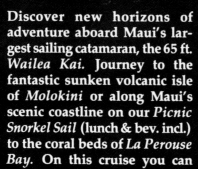

AMERICAN CUISINE
SEAFOOD

DAILY LUNCH 11-4
DAILY DINNER 5:30-9:30

WAILEA SHOPPING VILLAGE
WAILEA ALANUI DR.
WAILEA
879-6667

Ambrosia

CHICKEN MANETTI WITH CANNELONI SAUCE

2   WHOLE CHICKEN BREASTS (FOUR HALVES)
FLOUR (TO DREDGE)
SALT AND PEPPER (TO TASTE)
2   EGGS (MIXED WITH 2T WATER)
2   CUPS BREAD CRUMBS
OLIVE OIL (TO FRY)
4   PIECES SLICED HAM
1   PKG (10 OUNCES) SPINACH (CHOPPED)
4   SLICES JACK CHEESE

1. SEASON FLOUR WITH SALT AND PEPPER.
2. DREDGE CHICKEN IN SEASONED FLOUR; DIP IN EGG WASH MIXTURE, THEN COAT WITH BREAD CRUMBS.
3. IN A LARGE SKILLET WITH HOT OIL BROWN CHICKEN (10 MINUTES ON EACH SIDE).
4. PRE-HEAT OVEN TO 350 DEGREES.
5. PLACE CHICKEN IN A LARGE BAKING DISH.
6. PLACE 1 SLICE HAM, ONE-FOURTH OF THE SPINACH AND 1 SLICE CHEESE ON TOP OF EACH CHICKEN BREAST.
7. LADLE SAUCE OVER ALL AND BAKE 15 MINUTES IN 350 DEGREE OVEN.
8. SERVE WITH NOODLES AND A LARGE GREEN TOSSED SALAD.

PREPARATION: 10 MINUTES
COOKING/BAKING: 20/15 MINUTES
SERVES: 4

CANNELONI SAUCE

2	CUPS TOMATO SAUCE
1	t WHITE PEPPER
3	T BASIL
1	t LEA & PERRINS WORCESTERSHIRE SAUCE
1	CUP CHICKEN BROTH
3	T CORN STARCH

1. IN A LARGE SAUCE PAN BRING TOMATO SAUCE TO A BOIL.
2. ADD PEPPER, BASIL AND WORCESTERSHIRE SAUCE.
3. SHAKE CHICKEN BROTH AND CORN STARCH TOGETHER IN A JAR AND ADD TO SAUCE.
4. SIMMER SAUCE WHILE PREPARING CHICKEN MANETTI.

PREPARATION: 5 MINUTES
COOKING: 30-40 MINUTES

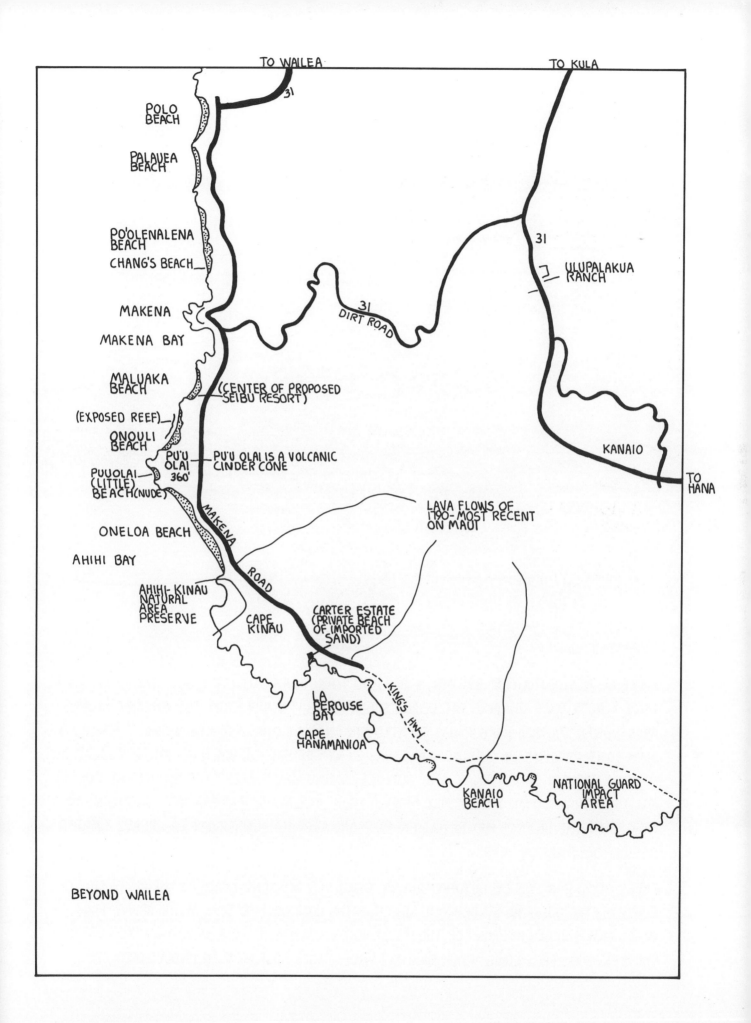

BEYOND WAILEA

BEYOND WAILEA

MAKENA. NOW BUT A FEW BUILDINGS, OLD AND TIRED, IN AN EXQUISITE SETTING, MAKENA WAS ONCE A BUSY PORT, SHIPPING CATTLE AND SUGAR BROUGHT DOWN FROM THE VOLCANIC SLOPES ABOVE. UNTIL KAHULUI HARBOR WAS CREATED MAKENA WAS ONE OF MAUI'S BIGGEST TOWNS. ITS ONLY CONTACT WITH THE OUTSIDE WORLD WAS BY WAY OF SHIP, SO WHEN ITS SHIPPING WAS LOST, MAKENA RAPIDLY FADED AWAY INTO SILENCE. WORLD WAR II BROKE THE SILENCE AS THE U·S. MILITARY TRANSFORMED THE COAST OF MAUI FROM MAALAEA TO MAKENA INTO A STAGING AREA! NOW, AGAIN, THE SILENCE MAY BE BROKEN AS PLANS ARE WELL-UNDERWAY TO CREATE A MAJOR RESORT DESTINATION HERE.

THREE GOOD BEACHES LIE BEYOND MAKENA: ONEULI (BLACK SAND BEACH, ON THE RIGHT SIDE OF PUU OLAI, THE VOLCANIC CINDER CONE WHICH IS THE DOMINANT FEATURE OF THE AREA); PUU OLAI BEACH (NUDE BEACH IN FRONT OF THE HILL); AND ONELOA BEACH (LONG BEACH) ON THE LEFT OF THE HILL, 3000 FEET LONG, AT LEAST 100 FEET WIDE-MAUI'S MOST POPULAR UNDEVELOPED BEACH!

LA PEROUSE

TO LAHAINA

PAST MAALAEA TOWARDS LAHAINA IS A FOUR MILE STRETCH OF PALI AND CURVES. THE OLD HIGHWAY WAS CALLED THE AMALFI DRIVE OF MAUI BECAUSE IT WAS NOTHING BUT CURVES! THE NEW ROAD ADDED A TUNNEL-THE FIRST IN HAWAII-AND TOOK OUT MANY OF THE CURVES. THE OLD ROADBED, THE BASIC PATHWAY THAT CARRIED SUCH PEOPLE AS MARK TWAIN AND HERMAN MELVILLE TO AND FROM LAHAINA (VIA HORSE) IS STILL VISIBLE. PAPAWAI POINT IS AN EXCELLENT PLACE TO VIEW THE OCEAN SHORELINES AND TO WHALE WATCH.

PAPALAUA STATE WAYSIDE PARK IS JUST PAST THE SEA CLIFFS. IT IS A VERY PLEASANT SPOT WITH SAFE WATERS. OLOWALU WAS THE SITE OF AN HISTORIC MASSACRE OF HAWAIIANS BY WHALERS AND A RETALIATORY ASSAULT BY HAWAIIANS, THE KIND OF BLOODY AFFAIR HISTORIANS OF HAWAII LOVE TO ENDLESSLY CHRONICLE. THROUGH THE CANE FIELDS BEHIND OLOWALU, A DIRT ROAD TAKES YOU TO SOME PETROGLYPHS. THE RAMP LEADING TO THE DRAWINGS HAS DECAYED AND MODERN "ARTISTS" HAVE DEFACED THE OLD, PRIMITIVE ETCHINGS- A COMMENTARY ON THEIR CURRENT STATUS!

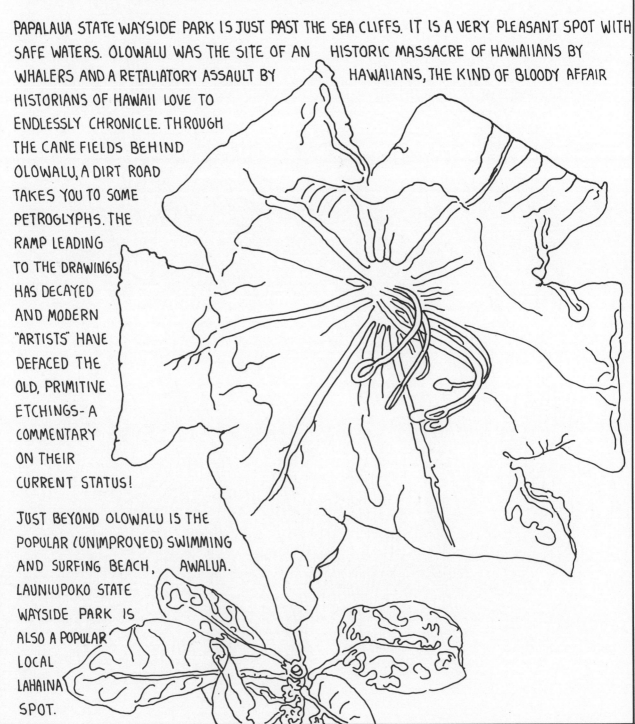

JUST BEYOND OLOWALU IS THE POPULAR (UNIMPROVED) SWIMMING AND SURFING BEACH, AWALUA. LAUNIUPOKO STATE WAYSIDE PARK IS ALSO A POPULAR LOCAL LAHAINA SPOT.

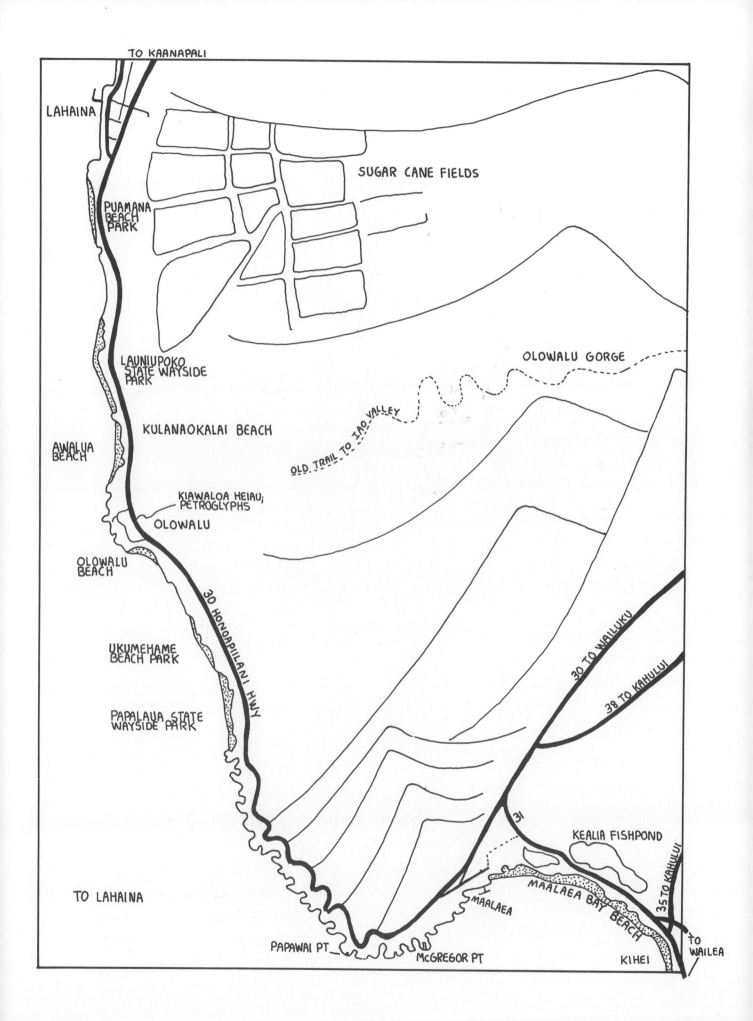

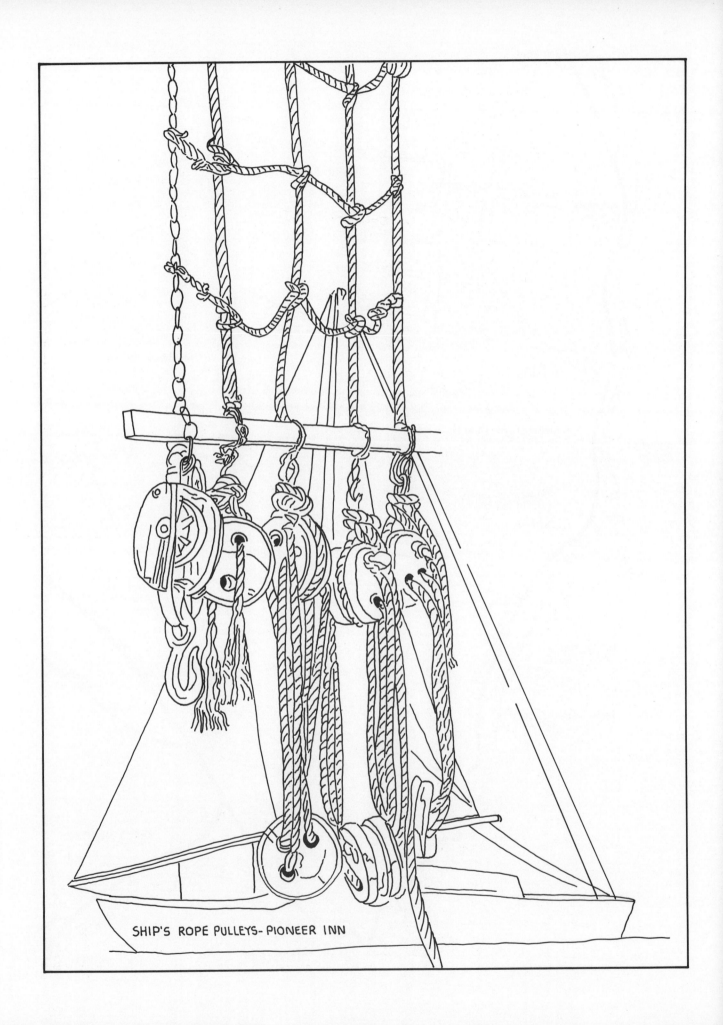

SHIP'S ROPE PULLEYS- PIONEER INN

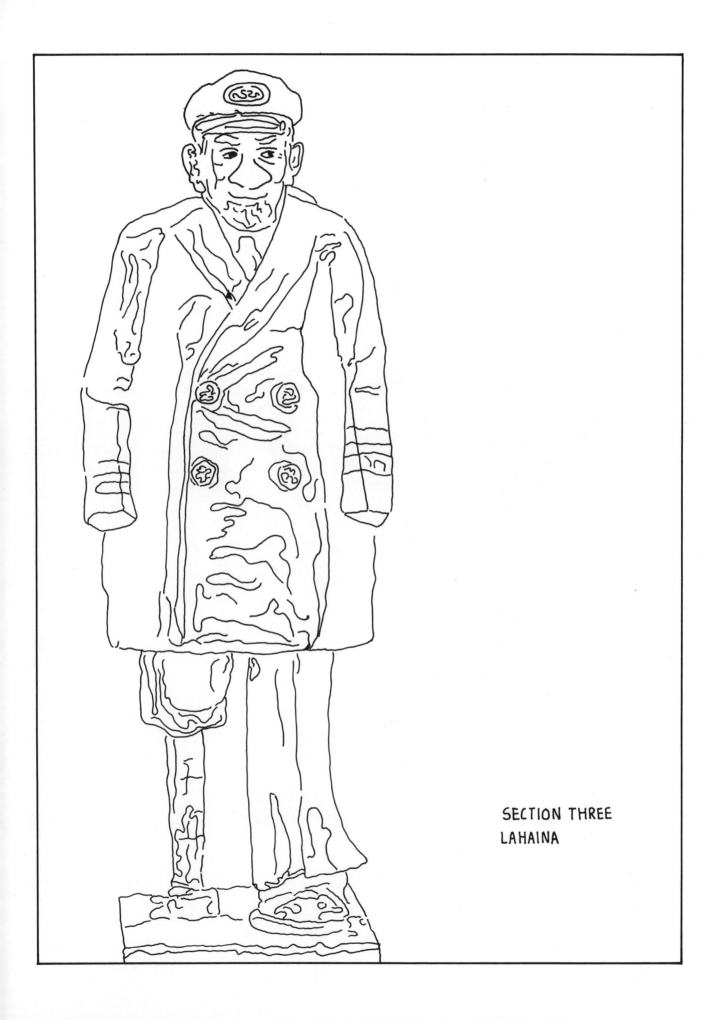

SECTION THREE
LAHAINA

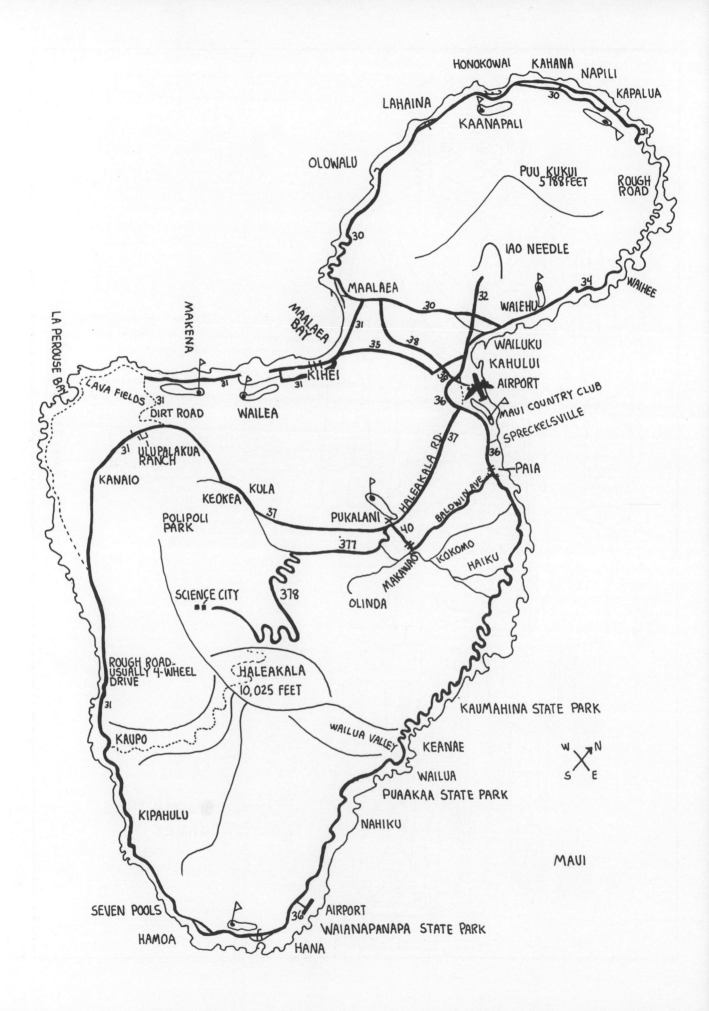

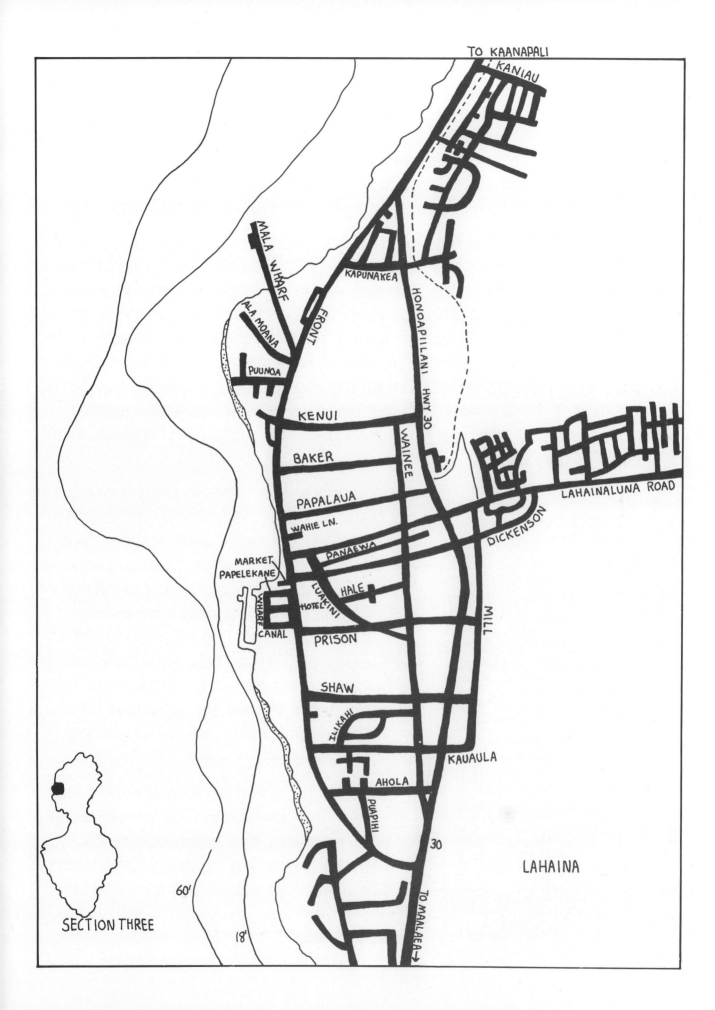

TO KAANAPALI

KANIAU

MALA WHARF

ALA MOANA

FRONT

KAPUNAKEA

HONOAPIILANI HWY 30

PUUNOA

KENUI

WAINEE

BAKER

PAPALAUA

WAHIE LN.

LAHAINALUNA ROAD

DICKENSON

PANAEWA

MARKET
PAPELEKANE

HALE

LUAKINI

HOTEL

WHARF

CANAL

PRISON

MILL

SHAW

ILIKAHI

KAUAULA

AHOLA

PUAPIHI

30

LAHAINA

60'

SECTION THREE

18'

TO MAALAEA→

LAHAINA

THE NAME SECOND ONLY TO WAIKIKI IN BEING SYNONYMOUS WITH "HAWAII"- LAHAINA! THE NAME MEANS, IF IT IS A REFERENCE TO THE WEATHER "MERCILESS SUN". IT MEANS "DAY (LA) OF SACRIFICE (HAINA)" IF IT IS A REFERENCE TO CERTAIN EXOTIC RELIGIOUS CUSTOMS OF THE AREA!

LAHAINA HAS BEEN A POPULAR PLACE FOR CENTURIES. MAUI IS A STORY OF CONSTANT VISITORS (AS TOLD SO WELL BY CUMMINS E. SPEAKMAN IN: MOWEE). FIRST CAME THE POLYNESIANS, WHO SAILED HERE IN THEIR DOUBLE-HULLED, 100 FOOT LONG SHIPS, SAILING OVER 2000 MILES OF OCEAN TO THE MOST ISOLATED ISLAND ARCHIPELAGO ON EARTH! THIS PERIOD OF IMMIGRATION WAS FROM 500 C.E. TO 1200, APPARENTLY. FOR WHATEVER REASONS - PERHAPS SKILLS OF NAVIGATION WERE LOST BECAUSE THERE WERE NO BETTER WORLDS TO DISCOVER- ALL CONTACT WITH THE OUTSIDE WORLD ENDED FOR 500 YEARS! THERE WAS NOT A WORD TO BE HEARD ABOUT THAT WORLD AND FINALLY THE CENTURIES OF ISOLATION PRODUCED DOUBT THAT ANYTHING ELSE EXISTED! THE ISLANDS *were* THE WORLD AND LAHAINA WAS ALWAYS A CENTER OF THAT WORLD!

BUT UNBEKNOWNST TO THESE LITTLE ISLAND KINGDOMS, BUSY WARRING AMONGST THEMSELVES TO SEE WHICH CHIEF WOULD WIN CONTROL OF ALL THE ISLANDS, THERE WAS AN OUTSIDE WORLD OF MIGHTY POLITICAL STATES WHOSE TENTACLES WERE STRETCHING TOWARDS THEM! THE **FLOOD** OF VISITORS FROM SUCH CONTACT WOULD QUICKLY AND FOREVER END THE LIFE THE ISLANDERS HAD KNOWN FOR GENERATIONS. FIRST CAME THE EUROPEAN ADVENTURERS AND TRADERS, THEN THE WHALERS, THE RANCHERS, MISSIONARIES, FIELD HANDS FROM ASIA AND EUROPE, MILITARY MEN, WORLD TRAVELERS IN SEARCH OF THE EXOTIC, LAND SPECULATORS AND THE TOURISTS.

LAHAINA HAS SEEN IT ALL! MANY OF MAUI'S RULERS LIVED HERE. KAMEHAMEHA I, THE FIRST RULER OVER ALL THE ISLANDS, MADE LAHAINA HIS HOME AND CAPITAL. LAHAINA WAS THE OFFICIAL CAPITAL FROM 1820-1845. THAT YEAR 1820 WAS ALSO SIGNIFICANT

BALDWIN HOUSE

BECAUSE THE NEWLY-DISCOVERED WHALING AREA SOUTH OF ALASKA CAUSED WHALING VESSELS TO COME SOUTH FOR REPAIRS AND REPROVISIONING. BY 1824, 100 SHIPS WERE VISITING LAHAINA PER YEAR. THE PEAK OF THE WHALING ERA (1845-1860; 1846: 429 SHIPS AT LAHAINA, 167 AT HONOLULU) SAW 100 SHIPS *at a time*! FOR A LITTLE TOWN OF 3500, TWO THOUSAND WHALERS ON-SHORE WAS QUITE A PROBLEM! THE TALES OF HELL-RAISING SAILORS ARE PART OF LAHAINA'S LORE, OF COURSE, AS THE SEA-MEN COLLIDED AGAINST A SLEEPY HAWAIIAN VILLAGE OF GRASS HUTS AND... MISSIONARIES!

WORD CAME TO NEW ENGLAND THAT THERE WERE SAVAGES IN THE PACIFIC WHICH NEEDED TO BE SAVED. MISSIONARIES SET OUT FROM CONNECTICUT AND THERE IS LITTLE DOUBT OF THEIR FAITH, AS NONE EXPECTED EVER AGAIN TO SEE HOME! THE FIRST MISSIONARIES ARRIVED IN 1823. THEY BUILT HOMES AS IF THEY WERE STILL HOME, HOWEVER! BALDWIN HOUSE (1834), IN THE CENTER OF TOWN, IS A RESTORED EXAMPLE. DESPITE THE CHAOS OF WHALING, LAHAINA BECAME THE CENTER OF LEARNING FOR HAWAII, DUE TO THE TEACHING OF THE MISSIONARIES AND THE EAGERNESS OF THE HAWAIIANS TO LEARN THE *palapala* (WRITING). HERE WERE EVOLVED THE FIRST LAWS OF THE KINGDOM.

BY 1871 MANY EVENTS CONSPIRED TO PUT AN END TO LAHAINA'S DAYS AS THE CAPITAL OF THE PACIFIC WHALING FLEETS: USE OF PETROLEUM, SHRINKAGE OF THE FLEET BECAUSE OF THE U.S. CIVIL WAR, AND A DISASTER IN ALASKAN WATERS. THE CENTER OF GOVERNMENT SHIFTED TO HONOLULU AND LAHAINA BECAME A SLEEPY BACKWATER INDEED! THE PLANTATION ERA CAME AND BOTH SUGAR AND PINEAPPLE PROVIDED QUIET, UNINSPIRED LIVLIHOODS- LAHAINA TOWN, THE SLOW, SLEEPY PLANTATION TOWN!

BUT IN THE LATE 1950s AMFAC (AMERICAN FACTORS, OWNERS OF PIONEER SUGAR MILL IN LAHAINA) BEGAN DEVELOPING SOMETHING NORTH OF TOWN CALLED "KAANAPALI BEACH RESORT," AND BY 1963 THE FIRST ROOMS AT THE ROYAL LAHAINA WERE READY. NO ONE EVER IMAGINED LAHAINA COULD CONTINUE ITS CENTURY-OLD NAP! IN 1964 LAHAINA BECAME A NATIONAL HISTORIC LANDMARK. THE IMPACT OF THE MASSIVE GROWTH AT KAANAPALI AND ELSEWHERE ON MAUI HAS BEEN FELT, BUT IT HAS BEEN ANTICIPATED AND PLANNED-FOR. BUSINESSPEOPLE, COUNTY OFFICIALS AND AMFAC HAVE SOUGHT TO CONTROL LAHAINA'S GROWTH AND THE LAHAINA RESTORATION FOUNDATION HAS CAREFULLY WATCHED-OVER THE HISTORICAL SITES.

RESTAURANTS: CHEZ PAUL IN OLOWALU (SIX MILES EAST OF TOWN); KIMO'S; ALEX'S HOLE IN THE WALL; LONGHI'S.

AS FOR SHOPS AND ACTIVITIES, IS IT EVEN CONCEIVABLE THAT SOMEONE COULD COME TO LAHAINA TOWN AND FIND NOTHING TO SEE OR DO OR BUY?

Chez Paul

RESTAURANT ✦ FRANÇAIS

FRENCH CUISINE
DINNER 5:30-10:30
RESERVATIONS
661-3843

OLOWALU VILLAGE
LAHAINA

CANARD LA PEROUSE

ONE 4-5 LB LONG ISLAND DUCKLING
SALT AND PEPPER (TO TASTE)
3   OZ OIL
1   CARROT (DICED)
1   ONION (DICED)
3   CELERY STICKS
3   BAY LEAVES
4   SPRIGS FRESH THYME
6   FRESH SAGE LEAVES
2   OZ BUTTER
2   OZ FLOUR
1|2 CUP SHERRY
3   SHALLOTS (DICED FINELY
1|4 CUP FRESH HEAVY CREAM
SALT AND PEPPER (TO TASTE)
1   T DIJON MUSTARD (OPTIONAL)
1   CUP BREAD CRUMBS
2|3 CUP GRUYERE CHEESE (GRATED)
1   OZ COLD MILK
DIJON MUSTARD (PAINT DUCK)

1. PREHEAT OVEN TO 500 DEGREES.
2. REMOVE WINGS, KNOBS ON TOP OF LEGS AND NECK OF DUCKLING. RESERVE FOR STOCK.
3. SALT AND PEPPER INSIDE CAVITY AND ON OUTSIDE OF DUCKLING.
4. IN ROASTING PAN ON A RAISED RACK, BAKE DUCK 45 MINUTES.
5. EMPTY FAT CAREFULLY AND LOWER OVEN TO 350 DEGREES. CONTINUE COOKING FOR ANOTHER 45 MINUTES.

continued...

(CONTINUED)

6. WHILE DUCK IS ROASTING, IN A LARGE SKILLET WITH HOT OIL, BROWN THE RESERVED DUCK PARTS (TEN MINUTES).

7. ADD CARROT, ONION, CELERY AND SAUTÉ UNTIL ONIONS ARE TRANSPARENT (ABOUT 5 MINUTES).

8. ADD FOUR CUPS WATER, SEASONINGS; BRING TO A BOIL. SIMMER FOR ONE HOUR, FREQUENTLY SKIMMING OFF FAT. REDUCE LIQUID TO 2 CUPS.

9. STRAIN THROUGH A CHINA CAP (A FINE SIEVE). SET ASIDE.

10. IN A MEDIUM SAUCEPAN, MAKE A ROUX WITH BUTTER AND FLOUR.

11. WISK IN STOCK. COOK, STIRRING OFTEN FOR 45 MINUTES.

12. IN ANOTHER SAUCEPAN PLACE SHERRY AND SHALLOTS, REDUCING TO 3 T OF LIQUID (7-10 MINUTES).

13. ADD SHERRY MIXTURE TO THICKENED STOCK AND SLOWLY ADD CREAM. COOK JUST TO THE BOILING POINT.

14. ADD SALT AND PEPPER AND, IF DESIRED, ADD THE MUSTARD. SET ASIDE. KEEP WARM.

15. MIX TOGETHER BREAD CRUMBS AND CHEESE. ADD MILK. BLEND TOGETHER WELL. SET ASIDE.

16. WHEN DUCKLING IS COOKED, REMOVE FROM OVEN. COOL.

17. WHEN COOLED, CUT IN HALF LENGTH-WISE. SEPARATE BREAST FROM LEG AND PLACE ON SERVING PLATTER.

18. PAINT DUCKLING WITH MUSTARD, USING A PASTRY BRUSH.

19. PRESS BREAD CRUMB MIXTURE ONTO THE PAINTED DUCKLING AND PLACE BACK ON ROASTING RACK IN PREHEATED 475 DEGREE OVEN UNTIL GOLDEN (ABOUT 12 MINUTES).

20. SERVE ON A PLATTER WITH THE SAUCE LADLED OVER TOP.

PREPARATION: 20-25 MINUTES
ROASTING: ONE HOUR AND 45 MINUTES
COOKING: TWO HOURS AND 15 MINUTES
SERVES: 6

THE OLD WATER TANK AT OLOWALU, BEHIND CHEZ PAUL RESTAURANT. THE DIRT ROAD IN FRONT OF THIS TANK GOING TOWARDS THE OLOWALU GAP, LEADS TO THE OLOWALU PETROGLYPHS (A FEW ROCK DRAWINGS, THOUGHT TO BE 250 YEARS OLD).

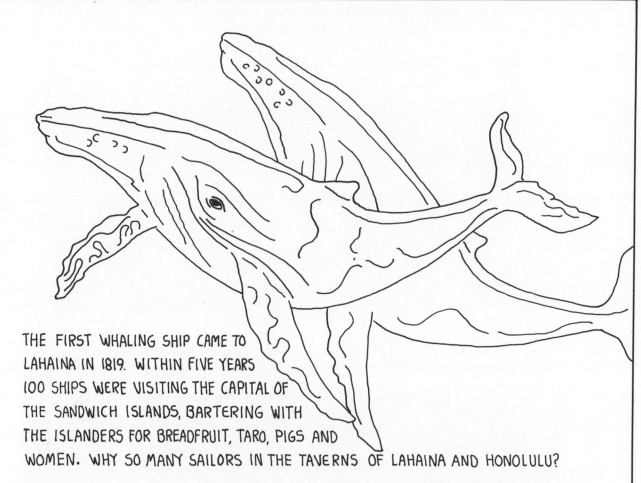

THE FIRST WHALING SHIP CAME TO
LAHAINA IN 1819. WITHIN FIVE YEARS
100 SHIPS WERE VISITING THE CAPITAL OF
THE SANDWICH ISLANDS, BARTERING WITH
THE ISLANDERS FOR BREADFRUIT, TARO, PIGS AND
WOMEN. WHY SO MANY SAILORS IN THE TAVERNS OF LAHAINA AND HONOLULU?

THE DISCOVERY OF THE SPERM WHALE AND ITS FEEDING GROUNDS IN THE SEAS SOUTH OF
ALASKA LURED THE WHALING FLEET INTO NORTH PACIFIC WATERS. WHALE OIL WAS USED
FOR LAMPS, SOAPS AND LEATHER TANNING, AND SPERM WHALES CONTAINED GREAT
AMOUNTS OF OIL. WITHIN THE HEAD OF SUCH A WHALE WAS FOUND A RESERVOIR OF
20-30 BARRELS OF OIL! SUCH A LARGE SUPPLY OF OIL LED TO GREATER USE OF IT AND
THUS TO GREATER HUNTING OF WHALES. SHIPS SAILED SOUTH TO MAUI FOR TWO GOOD
REASONS: TO REPROVISION THE SHIPS AND TO RECREATE THE CREWS. THE LAST SHIPS
CAME IN THE 1870s- THE GREAT WHALING BOOM LASTED LESS THAN 50 YEARS! THE U.S.
CIVIL WAR, NEW PACIFIC PORTS AND AN ARCTIC DISASTER (33 SHIPS BECAME TRAPPED
WITHIN A BAY AS ICE SEALED THE MOUTH) BROUGHT HAWAIIAN WHALING TO AN END.

THE HUMPBACK WHALE IS THE OFFICIAL STATE MARINE MAMMAL. IT WINTERS IN HAWAII
AND SUMMERS IN ALASKAN AND SIBERIAN WATERS. THE WHALES ARRIVE HERE BY
NOVEMBER AND DEPART BY MAY, WITH NEARLY 600 VISITING. THE WORLD'S POPULATION
OF HUMPBACKS IS THOUGHT TO BE 1000, AND IS APPROACHING EXTINCTION. THESE GENTLE,
40 TON, 45 FEET LONG GIANTS SPEND THEIR WINTER VACATION IN THE WATERS
BETWEEN MAUI AND KAHOOLAWE, LANAI AND MOLOKAI.

PIONEER INN

SAILING

THE SEA CHANNELS BETWEEN MAUI AND LANAI-MOLOKAI BRING YOU SIGHTS THAT ARE THE VERY ESSENCE OF HAWAII. THE EVER-CHANGING SCENE OF THE ISLANDS IS A MEMORY YOU'LL HAVE FOREVER! SAIL TO LITTLE LANAI'S MANELE BEACH, THE MOST POPULAR BEACH-PARK. STAY AN AFTERNOON OR STAY AT THE HOTEL LANAI FOR A DAY OR TWO AND EXPLORE THE ISLAND! OR SAIL TO BEAUTIFUL MOLOKAI TO KAUNAKAKAI, OR CRUISE PAST THE FABLED SEA CLIFFS AND VALLEYS OF THE NORTH SIDE! TRAVEL TO MOLOKINI, THE PARTIALLY SUBMERGED VOLCANO CRATER, NOW A MARINE PRESERVE. TOUR THE SHORELINE OF MAUI. TAKE A SUNSET CRUISE!

THERE IS ALSO ADVENTURE AS YOU SAIL THROUGH THE CRYSTAL WATERS. THERE ARE CORAL REEFS TO EXPLORE BY SNORKELING AND DIVING. DURING WINTER, ON A WHALE WATCH CRUISE YOU MAY SAIL RIGHT BESIDE THE GIANT HUMPBACK WHALES AT PLAY! MOST OF THE SAILING ACTIVITIES ORIGINATE FROM LAHAINA AND MAALAEA ALTHOUGH THEY MAY BE ARRANGED FROM ANY RESORT AREA. THIS ASSORTMENT OF YACHTS, SLOOPS, CATAMARANS, TRIMARANS AND "BOATS" WILL PROVIDE YOU WITH ALL THE EQUIPMENT, INSTRUCTION, LUNCH AND BEVERAGES YOUR ADVENTURE MAY REQUIRE!

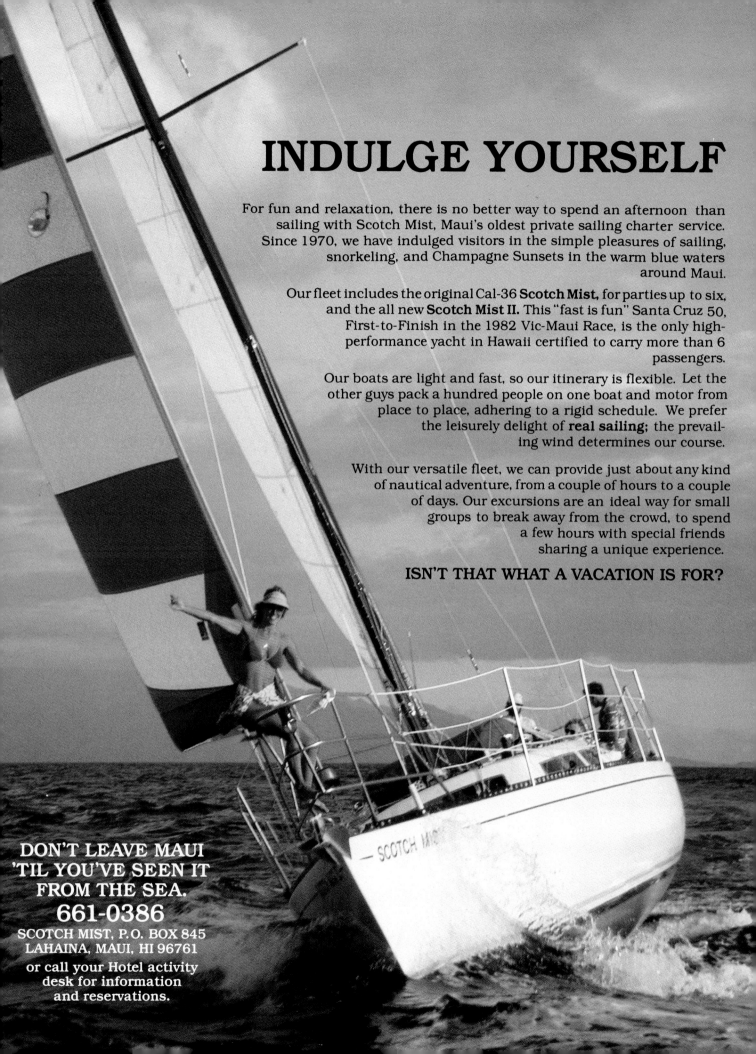

THE CARTHAGINIAN-
AS SEEN
FROM PIONEER INN

THE LAHAINA RESTORATION
FOUNDATION IS A NON-PROFIT
ORGANIZATION INCORPORATED
FOR EDUCATIONAL PURPOSES
AND FOR THE RESTORATION AND
PRESERVATION OF SITES IN LAHAINA.
IT RECEIVES NO GRANT MONIES
AND SUPPORTS ITSELF MAINLY BY
ADMISSION TO ITS MUSEUMS.
PROPERTIES OWNED OR MAIN-
TAINED ARE THE BALDWIN HOUSE,
MASTERS' READING ROOM, THE BARK CARTHAGINIAN
AND HALE PAI (THE PRINTING HOUSE) AT LAHAINALUNA.
EACH MUSEUM IS WORTHY OF YOUR TIME AND INTEREST!

MASTERS' READING ROOM

BALDWIN HOUSE-INTERIOR

THE VILLAGE GALLERIES HAVE BEEN SERVING THE ART COMMUNITY ON MAUI SINCE 1970. WITHIN THE THREE GALLERIES AN EXTENSIVE SELECTION OF THE FINEST ART WORKS BY LOCAL ARTISTS CAN BE FOUND. PICTURED HERE IS A RECENT OIL PAINTING BY MACARIO PASCUAL TITLED "WORKERS IN BLUE." OUR WHALER'S VILLAGE GALLERY IS LOCATED IN KAANAPALI NEXT TO THE MAUI SURF HOTEL. THE VILLAGE GALLERY-CANNERY IS ACROSS FROM THE OLD PINEAPPLE CANNERY IN LAHAINA AND OUR THIRD LOCATION, THE VILLAGE GALLERY-LAHAINA IS LOCATED BEHIND THE BALDWIN HOUSE.

AN EXCITING VARIETY OF OILS, WATERCOLORS, CERAMICS AND PRINTS BY HAWAII'S FINEST ARTISTS AWAIT YOUR VIEWING. OUR COURTEOUS AND KNOWLEDGEABLE SALES PEOPLE WILL BE HAPPY TO MEET YOU AND ANSWER YOUR QUESTIONS.

VILLAGE GALLERY WHALER'S VILLAGE. KAANAPALI. HOURS 930AM-9PM DAILY. 661-0196
VILLAGE GALLERY LAHAINA. 120 DICKENSON ST. HOURS 10AM-6PM DAILY. 661-4402
VILLAGE GALLERY AT THE CANNERY. 1287 FRONT ST. HOURS 10AM-6PM DAILY. 661-3280

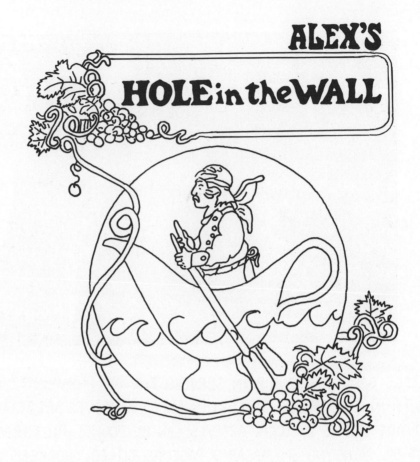

ALEX'S
HOLE in the WALL

ITALIAN AND CONTINENTAL CUISINE

DINNER 6-10 MONDAY-SATURDAY
834 FRONT STREET
(DOWN WAHIE LANE)
LAHAINA

RESERVATIONS
661-3197

LASAGNE VERDE

6   OZ. SPINACH LASAGNE NOODLES
OLIVE OIL (FOR FRYING)
1/2 LB. VEAL (GROUND)
2   PKG FROZEN SPINACH (THAWED
     AND DRAINED)
PEPPER (TO TASTE)
1   CLOVE GARLIC (CRUSHED)
1   LB. RICOTTA CHEESE
1   CUP PARMESAN CHEESE
2   t GARLIC POWDER
4   EGGS
1   LB. JACK CHEESE (GRATED)
1   LB. PROVOLONE OR MOZZARELLA
     (GRATED)
1   QUART SPAGHETTI SAUCE (USE YOUR
     OWN FAVORITE RECIPE)

1. IN A LARGE POT OF BOILING WATER, COOK NOODLES al-dente.
2. HEAT OIL IN MEDIUM SKILLET AND FRY VEAL UNTIL BROWN.
3. ADD SPINACH, PEPPER AND GARLIC; SAUTÉ TWO OR THREE MINUTES MORE.
4. SET ASIDE TO COOL.
Continued

ALEX'S

HOLE in the WALL

5. WHILE SPINACH MIXTURE IS COOLING MIX TOGETHER IN A LARGE BOWL 4 OZ. OF THE PARMESAN CHEESE, THE PEPPER AND GARLIC POWDER AND TWO OF THE EGGS. SET ASIDE.

6. IN A SEPARATE BOWL MIX TOGETHER JACK CHEESE, PROVOLONE AND THE REMAINING 4 OZ. OF PARMESAN CHEESE. SET ASIDE.

7. MIX THE REMAINING TWO EGGS INTO THE COOLED SPINACH MIXTURE. BLEND WELL.

8. IN A LARGE, FLAT CASSEROLE DISH ALTERNATE LAYERS OF NOODLES, SPINACH MIXTURE, RICOTTA MIXTURE, JACK CHEESE MIXTURE AND SAUCE UNTIL ALL INGREDIENTS ARE USED. LEAVE ENOUGH OF THE JACK CHEESE MIXTURE TO SPRINKLE ON TOP.

9. BAKE IN 350 DEGREE OVEN FOR 15-20 MINUTES OR UNTIL CHEESE IS A GOLDEN BROWN.

10. SERVE WITH A SPINACH SALAD.

PREPARATION: 30-40 MINUTES

SAUTÉ: 10 MINUTES

BAKING: 15-20 MINUTES

SERVES: 8-10

BALDWIN HOUSE

BALDWIN HOUSE

BALDWIN HOUSE STANDS ON THE LAHAINA TOWN SQUARE, THE TWO-STORY WHITE STUCCO RESIDENCE OF DWIGHT BALDWIN, A NATIVE OF DURHAM, CONNECTICUT, AND A MEMBER OF THE FOURTH COMPANY OF MISSIONARIES TO THE SANDWICH ISLANDS. BALDWIN HOUSE-RESTORED DISPLAYS WHAT LIFE WAS LIKE IN THE 1850s WHEN MISSIONARY- PHYSICIAN BALDWIN AND HIS FAMILY ENJOYED ITS SHELTER.

THE HOUSE ITSELF, THE HOUSEHOLD FURNITURE AND EQUIPMENT, THE AGED PHOTOGRAPHS AND ARTIFACTS, THE DISPLAYS AND LIBRARY, ALL PRESENT A VIVID PICTURE OF BUSY SANDWICH ISLES LIFE, PARTICULARLY THAT OF A MISSIONARY WHO WAS ALSO BOTH PHYSICIAN AND COMMUNITY FORCE. IN THIS HOME DR. BALDWIN RECEIVED MEMBERS OF THE ROYAL COURT, SHIP CAPTAINS, CONSULS AND WEARY TRAVELLERS. MASTERS AND SEAMEN WERE GIVEN THEIR OWN READING ROOM. THE FAITHFUL RESTORATION OF THE BALDWIN HOME IS BASED (CONT. ON ANCHOR PAGE)

OLD WHEELCHAIR
IN BALDWIN HOUSE

BALDWIN HOUSE

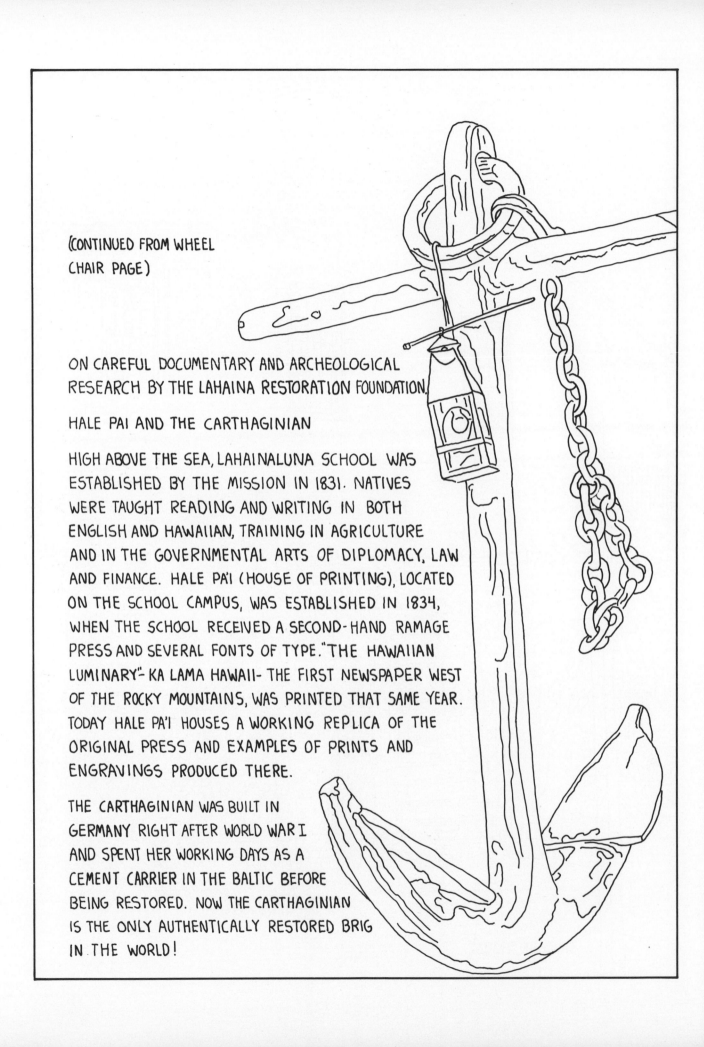

(CONTINUED FROM WHEEL
CHAIR PAGE)

ON CAREFUL DOCUMENTARY AND ARCHEOLOGICAL
RESEARCH BY THE LAHAINA RESTORATION FOUNDATION.

HALE PAI AND THE CARTHAGINIAN

HIGH ABOVE THE SEA, LAHAINALUNA SCHOOL WAS
ESTABLISHED BY THE MISSION IN 1831. NATIVES
WERE TAUGHT READING AND WRITING IN BOTH
ENGLISH AND HAWAIIAN, TRAINING IN AGRICULTURE
AND IN THE GOVERNMENTAL ARTS OF DIPLOMACY, LAW
AND FINANCE. HALE PA'I (HOUSE OF PRINTING), LOCATED
ON THE SCHOOL CAMPUS, WAS ESTABLISHED IN 1834,
WHEN THE SCHOOL RECEIVED A SECOND-HAND RAMAGE
PRESS AND SEVERAL FONTS OF TYPE."THE HAWAIIAN
LUMINARY"- KA LAMA HAWAII- THE FIRST NEWSPAPER WEST
OF THE ROCKY MOUNTAINS, WAS PRINTED THAT SAME YEAR.
TODAY HALE PA'I HOUSES A WORKING REPLICA OF THE
ORIGINAL PRESS AND EXAMPLES OF PRINTS AND
ENGRAVINGS PRODUCED THERE.

THE CARTHAGINIAN WAS BUILT IN
GERMANY RIGHT AFTER WORLD WAR I
AND SPENT HER WORKING DAYS AS A
CEMENT CARRIER IN THE BALTIC BEFORE
BEING RESTORED. NOW THE CARTHAGINIAN
IS THE ONLY AUTHENTICALLY RESTORED BRIG
IN THE WORLD!

HALE PA'I

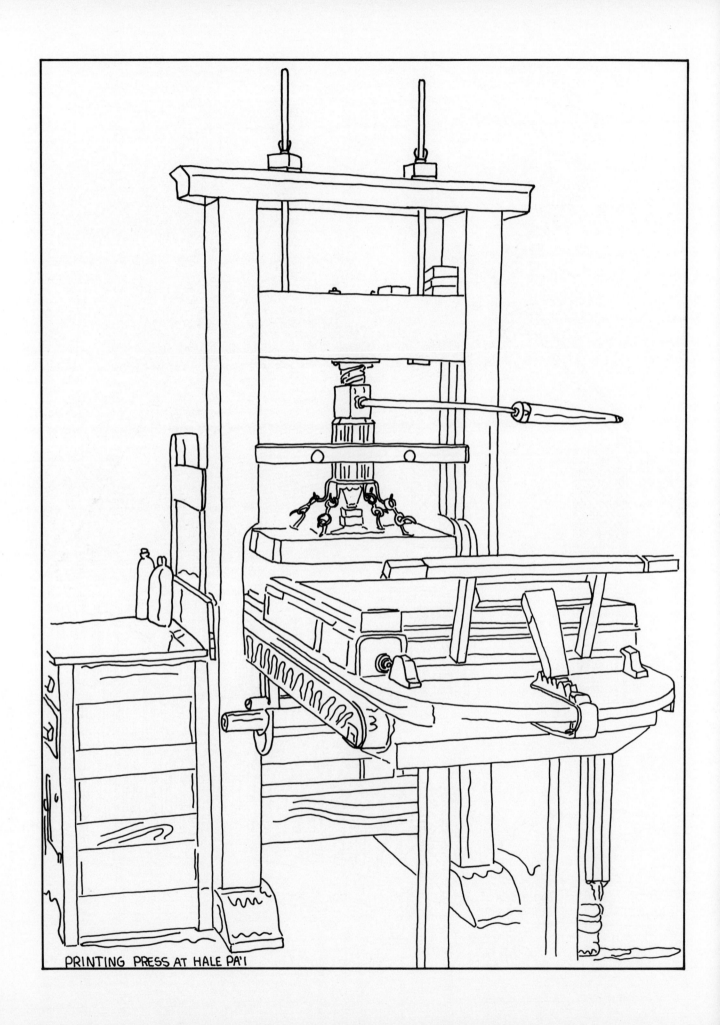

PRINTING PRESS AT HALE PA'I

for Winning Hands . . .

EMERALDS INTERNATIONAL INC.

858 Front Street   •   **Lahaina, Hawaii 96761**   •   **(808) 661-8705**

MJ March – Jeweller

AMERICAN CUISINE AND SEAFOOD

LUNCH 11:30-2:30 MONDAY-SATURDAY

DINNER 5-10:30

845 FRONT STREET

LAHAINA

661-4811

SCALLOPS

BUTTER (TO BASTE 8-OUNCE CASSEROLE DISH)
1/4   CUP SEASONED BREAD CRUMBS
2   T PARMESAN CHEESE
1/2   t PARSLEY FLAKES
1/2   LB SCALLOPS (LARGE)
1/4   t GARLIC SALT
3   OZ MELTED BUTTER

1. IN AN 8-OUNCE CASSEROLE DISH, BASTE INTERIOR WITH BUTTER
   TO PREVENT STICKING.
2. IN A SMALL BOWL MIX TOGETHER BREAD CRUMBS, PARMESAN
   CHEESE AND PARSLEY FLAKES. SET ASIDE.
3. SEASON SCALLOPS WITH GARLIC SALT. DIP INTO MELTED BUTTER.
   ROLL IN BREAD CRUMB MIXTURE.
4. PLACE BREADED SCALLOPS IN BUTTERED CASSEROLE DISH. POUR
   REMAINING BUTTER EVENLY OVER TOP.
5. BAKE IN A 350 DEGREE OVEN FOR 15 MINUTES UNTIL GOLDEN.

PREPARATION: 10 MINUTES
COOKING: 20 MINUTES
SERVES: ONE

ONIONS AND MUSHROOMS (APPETIZER)

1   SMALL MAUI ONION (OR SUBSTITUTE A SWEET ONION)
2   OZ BUTTER
4   OZ SMALL WHOLE BUTTON MUSHROOMS
1   T GARLIC POWDER
1   OZ CHABLIS WINE

1. REMOVE SKIN AND QUARTER ONION. BREAK INTO
   SEGMENTED LAYERS. (SET ASIDE.)
2. IN A MEDIUM SKILLET MELT BUTTER; OVER MEDIUM-HIGH
   FLAME SAUTÉ MUSHROOMS AND ONIONS IN BUTTER,
   STIRRING CONSTANTLY TO AVOID SCORCHING (5 MIN.).
3. ADD REMAINING INGREDIENTS AND COOK UNTIL
   ONIONS ARE TRANSLUCENT (5-7 MIN.).

PREPARATION: 5 MINUTES
COOKING: 10-12 MINUTES
SERVES: 4

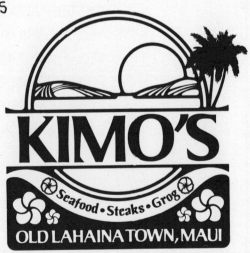

Apparels of Pauline

697 Front Street
Lahaina, Hawaii 96761
Phone: (808) 661-4774

2132 Kuhio Ave.
Honolulu, Hawaii 96815
Phone: (808) 922-5274

LAHAINA ARTS SOCIETY

THE LAHAINA ARTS SOCIETY WAS FOUNDED IN 1966 AND IS CURRENTLY LOCATED IN THE OLD COURTHOUSE BUILDING BEHIND THE BANYAN TREE ON THE WATERFRONT. IT IS THE ONLY ART ORGANIZATION IN HAWAII WHICH AFFORDS ITS MEMBERS A CONTINUING OPPORTUNITY TO EXHIBIT THEIR WORKS. IT IS A NON-PROFIT ORGANIZATION SUPPORTED ENTIRELY THROUGH ITS MEMBERSHIP AND BY A COUNTY OF MAUI DONATION OF GALLERY AND WORKSHOP SPACES.

THE TWO GALLERIES ARE OPEN DAILY FROM 10 TO 4 WITH A FEATURED SHOW IN THE MAIN GALLERY AND A GENERAL MEMBERSHIP SHOW IN THE OLD JAIL GALLERY. INCIDENTALLY, THERE IS ONLY ONE OTHER KNOWN GALLERY IN THE USA WHICH WAS ORIGINALLY A JAIL!

THE LAHAINA ARTS SOCIETY IS COMMITTED TO ENHANCING PUBLIC APPRECIATION OF THE ARTS. EACH YEAR MEMBERS DONATE ART-WORKS WHICH ARE AUCTION-ED OFF. THE FUNDS SO RAISED BECOME A SCHOLAR-SHIP WHICH IS AWARDED TO A DESERVING HIGH SCHOOL SENIOR.

THE TWO GALLERIES ARE OPEN TO THE PUBLIC AND THE ARTS SOCIETY WELCOMES YOUR VISIT. ALSO, MEMBER ARTISTS DEMONSTRATE AND EXHIBIT THEIR WORK EVERY WEEKEND AND ON HOLIDAYS OUTSIDE UNDER THE BANYAN TREE. GOOD LOCAL ART!

DRAWING FROM PAINTING IN OLD JAIL BY "APOLLO"

A LAHAINA PATIO

ECLECTIC FRENCH AND ITALIAN CUISINE
"ALWAYS OPEN":
BREAKFAST 7:30-11:30
LUNCH 11:30-4
DINNER 5-10

888 FRONT STREET
LAHAINA
667-2288

CASUALLY ELEGANT

CHICKEN MARSALA
(REFRIGERATE 3 HOURS)

2	WHOLE CHICKEN BREASTS (CUT INTO 4 HALVES)
2	EGGS (BEATEN
1	CUP PARMESAN CHEESE
4	OZ BUTTER
1\2	CUP OLIVE OIL
1\2	CUP DRY MARSALA
1	LEMON (CUT IN HALF)
2	OZ MUSHROOMS (SLICED)
1	t BASIL
1	t PARSLEY
4	SLICES FRENCH BREAD (TOASTED)

1. DIP CHICKEN BREASTS IN EGGS, THEN COAT WITH CHEESE. REFRIGERATE THREE HOURS.
2. IN LARGE SKILLET, MELT BUTTER. ADD OIL AND SAUTÉ CHICKEN BREASTS 5-7 MINUTES EACH SIDE.
3. ADD WINE, JUICE OF ONE-HALF LEMON, AND SIMMER 2-3 MINUTES.
4. ADD MUSHROOMS, BASIL AND PARSLEY. COOK 2 MORE MINUTES.
5. SERVE ON TOASTED FRENCH BREAD.

PREPARATION: 10 MINUTES
REFRIGERATION: 3 HOURS
COOKING: 15-20 MINUTES
SERVES: 4

MACADAMIA NUT PIE

1	9-INCH DEEP DISH PIE CRUST OR PUFF PASTRY
4	EGGS
1-1/2	CUPS BROWN SUGAR
1	CUP LIGHT KARO SYRUP
1/4	CUP MELTED BUTTER
1	CUP WHOLE MACADAMIA NUTS
1	CUP DICED MACADAMIA NUTS

1. PREHEAT OVEN TO 350 DEGREES.
2. IN A MEDIUM MIXING BOWL, MIX TOGETHER EGGS, SUGAR AND SYRUP WITH WARM MELTED BUTTER. SET ASIDE.
3. PLACE NUTS INTO PIE SHELL.
4. POUR EGG MIXTURE OVER NUTS.
5. BAKE FOR 45 MINUTES. LET COOL FOR ONE HOUR.
6. SERVE LONGHI-STYLE WITH HOMEMADE WHIPPED CREAM.

PREPARATION: 15-20 MINUTES
COOKING: 45 MINUTES
YIELD: ONE 9-INCH PIE

(TIME DOES NOT INCLUDE MAKING PIE CRUST.)

LONGHI'S

THE ROYAL LAHAINA

SECTION FOUR
KAANAPALI

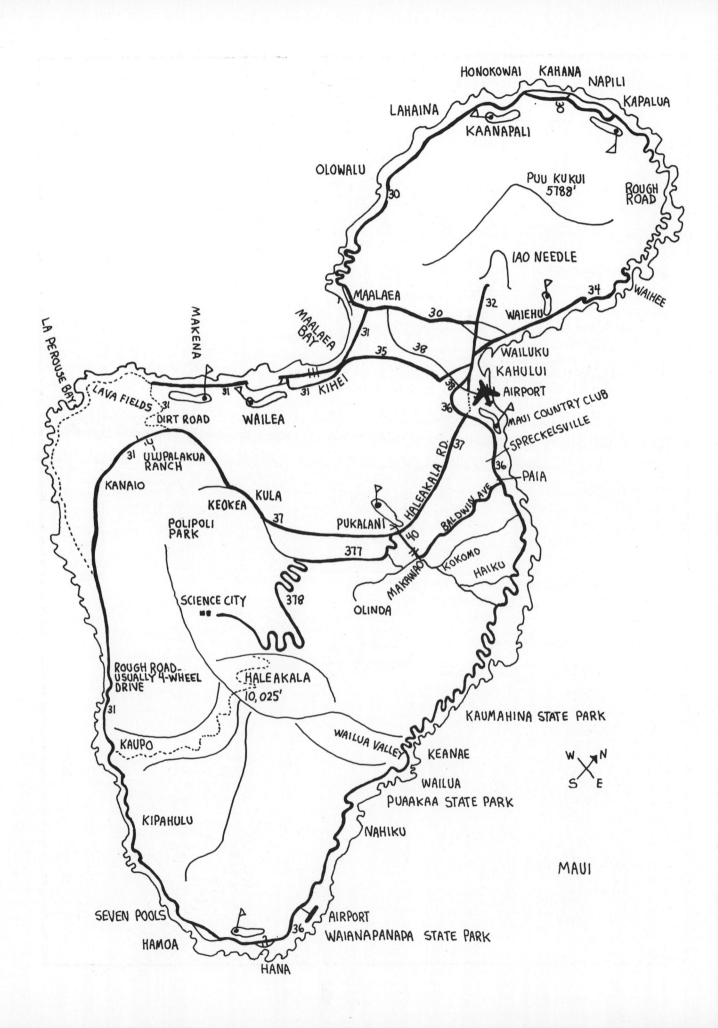

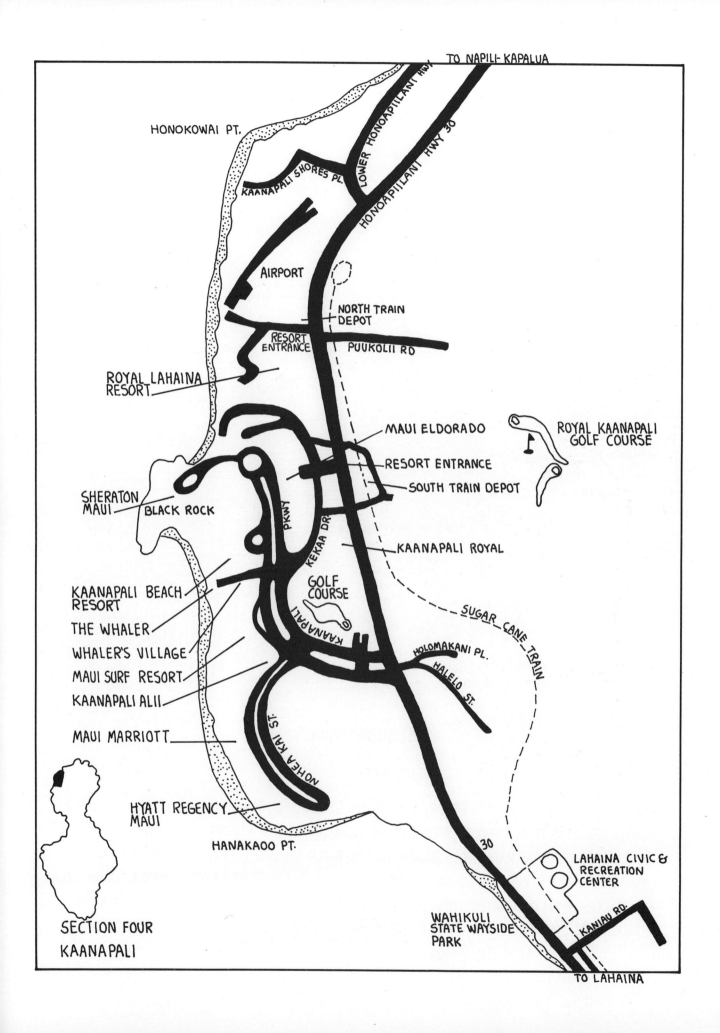

TO NAPILI-KAPALUA

HONOKOWAI PT.

KAANAPALI SHORES PL.

LOWER HONOAPIILANI HWY

HONOAPIILANI HWY 30

AIRPORT

NORTH TRAIN DEPOT

RESORT ENTRANCE

PUUKOLII RD

ROYAL LAHAINA RESORT

MAUI ELDORADO

RESORT ENTRANCE

SOUTH TRAIN DEPOT

ROYAL KAANAPALI GOLF COURSE

SHERATON MAUI

BLACK ROCK

PKWY

KEKAA DR.

KAANAPALI ROYAL

KAANAPALI BEACH RESORT

THE WHALER

WHALER'S VILLAGE

MAUI SURF RESORT

KAANAPALI ALII

KAANAPALI

GOLF COURSE

SUGAR CANE TRAIN

HOLOMAKANI PL.

HALELO ST.

MAUI MARRIOTT

NOHEA KAI ST.

HYATT REGENCY MAUI

HANAKAOO PT.

30

WAHIKULI STATE WAYSIDE PARK

LAHAINA CIVIC & RECREATION CENTER

KANIAU RD.

SECTION FOUR
KAANAPALI

TO LAHAINA

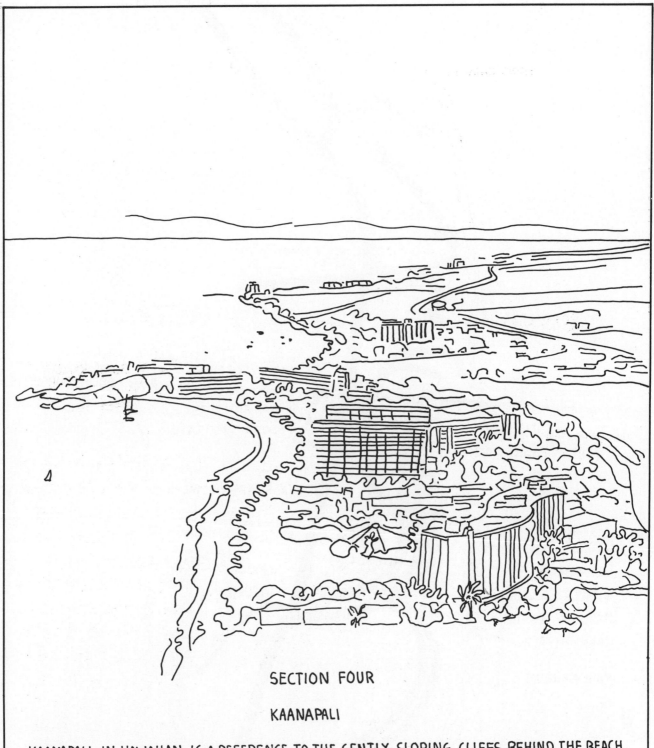

SECTION FOUR

KAANAPALI

KAANAPALI, IN HAWAIIAN, IS A REFERENCE TO THE GENTLY-SLOPING CLIFFS BEHIND THE BEACH. IN ENGLISH, IT IS A REFERENCE TO ONE OF THE WORLD'S GREAT RESORT DESTINATIONS! THE CENTRAL FEATURE OF KAANAPALI BEACH IS THE BLACK VOLCANIC CINDER CONE, PUU KEKAA (KNOWN AS BLACK ROCK TO LOCALS), NOW SITE OF THE SHERATON MAUI COMPLEX. THIS AREA HAS ALWAYS BEEN CULTIVATED, FIRST BY THE POLYNESIANS WHO, OVER THE CENTURIES BECAME "HAWAIIANS". THESE NATIVES GREW MANY THINGS, INCLUDING TARO, BREADFRUIT, MANGOS,

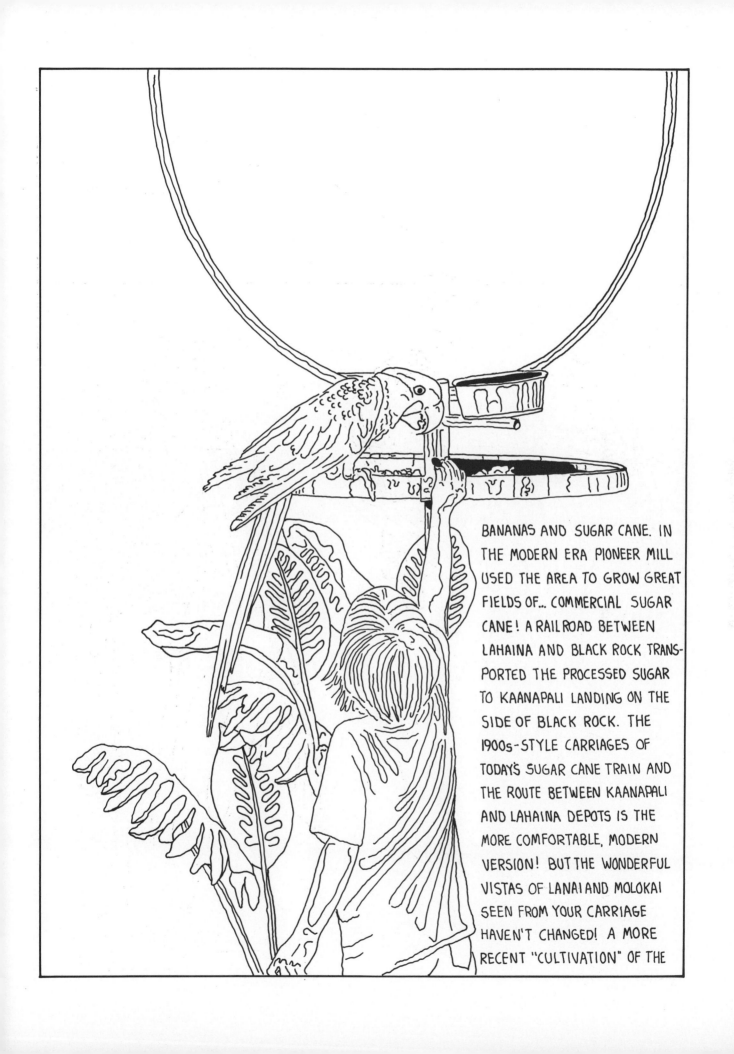

BANANAS AND SUGAR CANE. IN
THE MODERN ERA PIONEER MILL
USED THE AREA TO GROW GREAT
FIELDS OF... COMMERCIAL SUGAR
CANE! A RAILROAD BETWEEN
LAHAINA AND BLACK ROCK TRANS-
PORTED THE PROCESSED SUGAR
TO KAANAPALI LANDING ON THE
SIDE OF BLACK ROCK. THE
1900s-STYLE CARRIAGES OF
TODAY'S SUGAR CANE TRAIN AND
THE ROUTE BETWEEN KAANAPALI
AND LAHAINA DEPOTS IS THE
MORE COMFORTABLE, MODERN
VERSION! BUT THE WONDERFUL
VISTAS OF LANAI AND MOLOKAI
SEEN FROM YOUR CARRIAGE
HAVEN'T CHANGED! A MORE
RECENT "CULTIVATION" OF THE

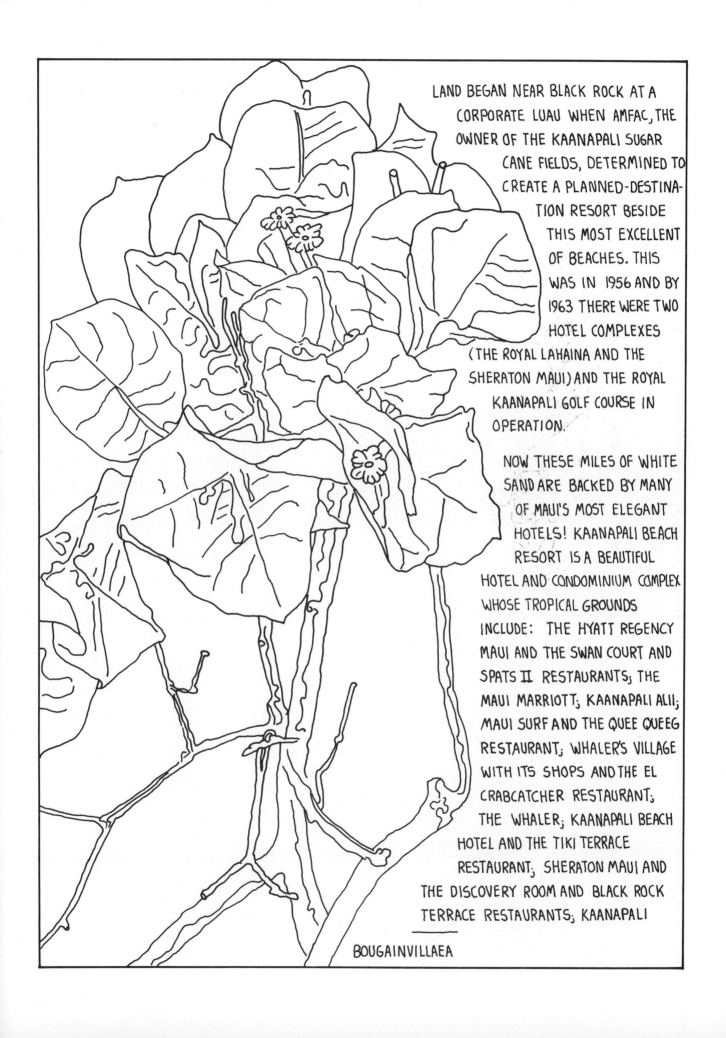

LAND BEGAN NEAR BLACK ROCK AT A CORPORATE LUAU WHEN AMFAC, THE OWNER OF THE KAANAPALI SUGAR CANE FIELDS, DETERMINED TO CREATE A PLANNED-DESTINATION RESORT BESIDE THIS MOST EXCELLENT OF BEACHES. THIS WAS IN 1956 AND BY 1963 THERE WERE TWO HOTEL COMPLEXES (THE ROYAL LAHAINA AND THE SHERATON MAUI) AND THE ROYAL KAANAPALI GOLF COURSE IN OPERATION.

NOW THESE MILES OF WHITE SAND ARE BACKED BY MANY OF MAUI'S MOST ELEGANT HOTELS! KAANAPALI BEACH RESORT IS A BEAUTIFUL HOTEL AND CONDOMINIUM COMPLEX WHOSE TROPICAL GROUNDS INCLUDE: THE HYATT REGENCY MAUI AND THE SWAN COURT AND SPATS II RESTAURANTS; THE MAUI MARRIOTT; KAANAPALI ALII; MAUI SURF AND THE QUEE QUEEG RESTAURANT; WHALER'S VILLAGE WITH ITS SHOPS AND THE EL CRABCATCHER RESTAURANT; THE WHALER; KAANAPALI BEACH HOTEL AND THE TIKI TERRACE RESTAURANT; SHERATON MAUI AND THE DISCOVERY ROOM AND BLACK ROCK TERRACE RESTAURANTS; KAANAPALI

BOUGAINVILLAEA

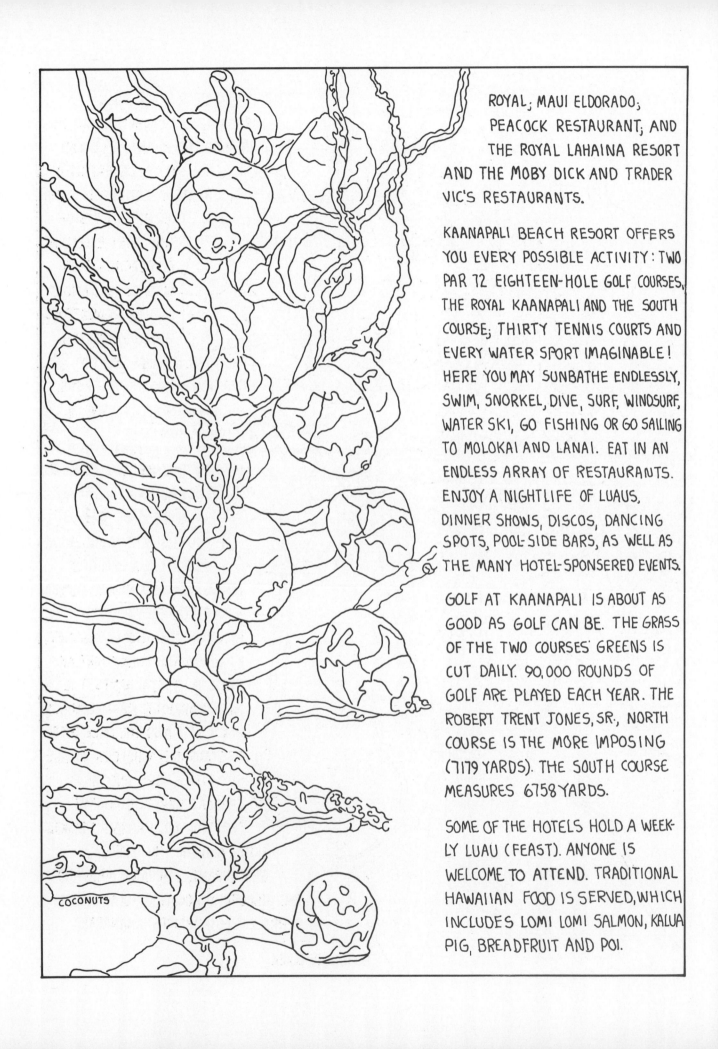

COCONUTS

ROYAL; MAUI ELDORADO;
PEACOCK RESTAURANT; AND
THE ROYAL LAHAINA RESORT
AND THE MOBY DICK AND TRADER
VIC'S RESTAURANTS.

KAANAPALI BEACH RESORT OFFERS
YOU EVERY POSSIBLE ACTIVITY: TWO
PAR 72 EIGHTEEN-HOLE GOLF COURSES,
THE ROYAL KAANAPALI AND THE SOUTH
COURSE; THIRTY TENNIS COURTS AND
EVERY WATER SPORT IMAGINABLE!
HERE YOU MAY SUNBATHE ENDLESSLY,
SWIM, SNORKEL, DIVE, SURF, WINDSURF,
WATER SKI, GO FISHING OR GO SAILING
TO MOLOKAI AND LANAI. EAT IN AN
ENDLESS ARRAY OF RESTAURANTS.
ENJOY A NIGHTLIFE OF LUAUS,
DINNER SHOWS, DISCOS, DANCING
SPOTS, POOL-SIDE BARS, AS WELL AS
THE MANY HOTEL-SPONSERED EVENTS.

GOLF AT KAANAPALI IS ABOUT AS
GOOD AS GOLF CAN BE. THE GRASS
OF THE TWO COURSES' GREENS IS
CUT DAILY. 90,000 ROUNDS OF
GOLF ARE PLAYED EACH YEAR. THE
ROBERT TRENT JONES, SR., NORTH
COURSE IS THE MORE IMPOSING
(7179 YARDS). THE SOUTH COURSE
MEASURES 6758 YARDS.

SOME OF THE HOTELS HOLD A WEEK-
LY LUAU (FEAST). ANYONE IS
WELCOME TO ATTEND. TRADITIONAL
HAWAIIAN FOOD IS SERVED, WHICH
INCLUDES LOMI LOMI SALMON, KALUA
PIG, BREADFRUIT AND POI.

HYATT REGENCY MAUI

SWAN COURT

CONTINENTAL CUISINE
BREAKFAST BUFFET 6:30-11
DINNER 6-9:30
RESERVATIONS
667-7474

LOCATED IN THE
HYATT REGENCY MAUI
KAANAPALI

SWAN COURT

WHITE SWAN

SPECIALTY OF SWAN COURT

1|2   SHOT AMARETTO
1|2   SHOT SCOTCH
1|2   SHOT COGNAC
1|2   PINT VANILLA ICE CREAM
      (SWAN COURT USES HAAGEN DAZS)
1|2   CUP ICE
SPLASH OF SWEET SYRUP
NUTMEG (GARNISH)

1. PLACE ALL INGREDIENTS IN A BLENDER (ICE CAN BE VARIED DEPENDING
   ON DESIRED THICKNESS.
2. POUR INTO 16-OUNCE LONG-STEMMED
   GLASS. SPRINKLE NUTMEG ON TOP.

PREPARATION: 1 MIN.
SERVES: ONE

HUKILAU IN GINGER-LEMON BUTTER

1-1/2 LBS FRESH WHITE FISH
SALT AND PEPPER (TO TASTE)
FLOUR (TO DREDGE)
1   EGG (BEATEN)
2   OZ BUTTER (CLARIFIED)
GINGER-LEMON BUTTER:
2   T FRESH GINGER (FINELY CHOPPED)
1/4 CUP WHITE WINE
JUICE OF ONE-HALF LEMON
4   OZ BUTTER

1. PREHEAT OVEN TO 350 DEGREES.
2. SEASON FISH WITH SALT AND PEPPER. DREDGE IN FLOUR AND DIP IN EGG.
3. IN A MEDIUM SKILLET, SAUTÉ IN HOT BUTTER UNTIL BROWN (2-3 MINUTES).
4. PLACE IN OVEN AND BAKE 8-10 MINUTES.

GINGER-LEMON BUTTER:

1. PLACE GINGER IN SMALL SAUCEPAN WITH WINE AND LEMON JUICE. BRING TO A BOIL.
2. REMOVE FROM HEAT AND ADD BUTTER. WHEN BUTTER IS MELTED, SAUCE SHOULD BE CONSISTENCY OF CREAM.
3. POUR OVER FISH AND SERVE.

PREPARATION: 10 MINUTES
BAKING: 8-10 MINUTES
SAUTÉING: 2-3 MINUTES
COOKING: 2 MINUTES
SERVES: 4

SWAN COURT

HYATT REGENCY MAUI

ITALIAN CUISINE
DINNER 6-9:30
DISCO 9:30-1 AM
RESERVATIONS
667-7474

LOCATED IN THE
HYATT REGENCY MAUI
KAANAPALI

LINGUINE CON SCAMPI

1/2	LB PRAWNS (PEELED, DEVEINED)	

1/2   LB PRAWNS (PEELED, DEVEINED)
2   T OLIVE OIL
3   OZ BUTTER
2   CLOVES OF GARLIC (MINCED)
2   T SHALLOTS (MINCED)
2   OZ RED WINE
PINCH OF CRUSHED RED PEPPERS
SALT AND PEPPER (TO TASTE)
1   t FRESH THYME (1/4 t IF NOT FRESH)
1   t OREGANO
3   T LEMON JUICE
1   LB FRESH SPINACH LINGUINE

1. PUT WATER ON TO BOIL FOR COOKING PASTA.
2. CUT PRAWNS INTO SMALL PIECES. SAUTÉ QUICKLY IN OLIVE OIL AND BUTTER UNTIL COLOR BEGINS TO CHANGE (1-2 MINUTES).
3. ADD GARLIC, SHALLOTS. COOK 2-3 MINUTES.
4. DEGLAZE WITH WHITE WINE. ADD SEASONINGS AND LEMON JUICE. COOK TOGETHER UNTIL PRAWNS ARE DONE.
5. COOK PASTA IN BOILING WATER UNTIL AL DENTE.
6. TOSS PRAWNS WITH PASTA. SERVE IMMEDIATELY.

PREPARATION: 5 MINUTES
COOKING: 12-15 MINUTES
SERVES: 4

SPINACH SALAD WITH DRESSING

DRESSING:
4   EGG YOLKS
2   T DIJON MUSTARD
3|4 CUP OLIVE OIL
1   T OREGANO LEAVES
4   T RED WINE VINEGAR
2   DASHES ANGOSTURA BITTERS
2   T GRENADINE SYRUP
SALT AND PEPPER TO TASTE

1. THOROUGHLY MIX TOGETHER EGG YOLKS, MUSTARD AND OREGANO.
2. SLOWLY ADD OIL, VINEGAR, BITTERS AND GRENADINE. SEASON.

PREPARATION: 5 MINUTES
YIELD: 1-1|2 CUPS

SPINACH SALAD:
1   LB FRESH SPINACH LEAVES
1|4 LB MUSHROOMS (THINLY SLICED)
1|4 LB PROSCUITTO HAM (JULIENNE)
2   OZ BACON BITS
     (4 STRIPS COOKED)
     CUP PARMESAN CHEESE
1   SMALL ONION (THINLY SLICED)
2   EGGS (HARD BOILED)

TOSS TOGETHER AND SERVE WITH PREPARED DRESSING.

PREPARATION: 5 MINUTES
YIELD: 1-1|2 CUPS

ENTRY TO QUEE QUEEG

THE QueeQueg

PRAWNS KUSHIYAKI

MARINADE

4	CLOVES GARLIC (CRUSHED)
2	T FRESH GINGER (GRATED)
1/4	CUP SHOYU (SOY SAUCE)
1/2	CUP PALE DRY SHERRY
1/2	CUP PINEAPPLE JUICE
3/4	CUP BROWN SUGAR
2	T SESAME OIL
1/4	CUP PREPARED BLACK BEAN SAUCE
10	PRAWNS
1	LARGE BELL PEPPER (IN 8 PIECES)
8	1-INCH PIECES FRESH PINEAPPLE
2	MUSHROOM CAPS

1. PLACE ALL EIGHT MARINADE INGREDIENTS IN A BOWL. MIX WELL.
2. MARINATE PRAWNS, PEPPER AND PINEAPPLE PIECES AND MUSHROOM CAPS FOR AT LEAST ONE HOUR.
3. REMOVE FROM MARINADE AND ASSEMBLE PIECES ON SKEWERS. INTERLACE PRAWNS (2 PER SKEWER) WITH BELL PEPPER AND PINEAPPLE CHUNKS. TOP WITH MUSHROOM CAPS.
4. BROIL SKEWERS UNTIL DONE (10-12 MIN.). HEAT REMAINING SAUCE AND SERVE ON SIDE.

PREPARATION: 20-25 MINUTES
COOKING: 10-12 MINUTES
YIELDS: 2 SKEWERS

THE QueeQueg

SCALLOPS MANDALAY

2   T PEANUT OIL
DASH OF SALT
1/2 t FRESH GINGER (MINCED)
1/2 t GARLIC (MINCED)
5   MEDIUM SCALLOPS
1/4 CUP DRY VERMOUTH
GREEN ONIONS (GARNISH), JULIENNE

1. IN A LARGE SKILLET HEAT OIL. STIR-FRY SALT, GINGER AND GARLIC.
2. ADD SCALLOPS AND STIR-FRY (2-3 MINUTES).
3. ADD VERMOUTH. BRING TO A BOIL AND COOK 3-4 MINUTES LONGER.
4. MAKE A CORN STARCH PASTE (ONE-HALF t. CORN STARCH TO ONE T. WATER)
   AND THICKEN THE WINE SAUCE.
5. TOP WITH GREEN ONIONS.
6. SERVE WITH RICE.

PREPARATION: 5 MINUTES
COOKING: 10 MINUTES
SERVES: ONE

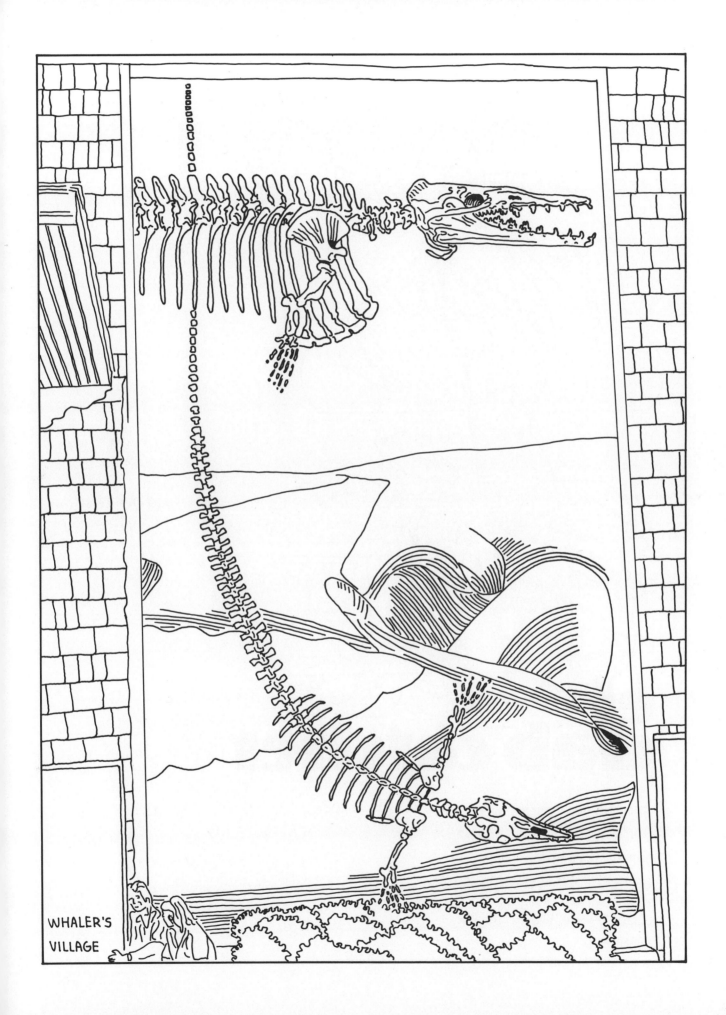

WHALER'S
VILLAGE

el crab catcher

SEAFOOD AND MEXICAN SPECIALTIES
LUNCH 11:30-3
DINNER 5:30-10:30
661-4423 FOR RESERVATIONS

LOCATED IN WHALER'S VILLAGE
KAANAPALI

el crab catcher

LOBSTER THERMIDOR

6   LOBSTERS (1|2 LB. EACH)
2   T TARRAGON
3   T RED WINE VINEGAR
1   CUP SHERRY
4   CUPS MORNEY SAUCE*
2   CUPS HOLLANDAISE SAUCE*
1   CUP PARMESAN CHEESE

1. CRACK LOBSTER SHELLS IN HALF AND REMOVE MEAT. RETAIN SHELLS. CUBE MEAT.
2. BOIL TARRAGON IN VINEGAR UNTIL NO LIQUID REMAINS. SET ASIDE.
3. POACH LOBSTER MEAT IN SHERRY AND ENOUGH WATER TO COVER MEAT. UNDER-COOK SLIGHTLY.
4. DRAIN. DISCARD LIQUID. ADD MORNEY SAUCE TO MEAT AND BRING TO A BOIL. COOK TWO MINUTES.
5. RE-STUFF LOBSTER SHELLS WITH MEAT AND SAUCE MIXTURE.
6. TOP WITH HOLLANDAISE SAUCE AND PARMESAN CHEESE.
7. BROIL IN OVEN UNTIL BROWNED
8. SERVE WITH WILD RICE AND TOSSED GREEN SALAD.

PREPARATION: 15 MINUTES
COOKING: 12-15 MINUTES
SERVES: 6
*USE YOUR OWN FAVORITE RECIPE OR BUY PREPARED SAUCE.

el crab catcher

GRAND MARNIER AND PAPAYA SOUFFLÉ

6	SOUFFLÉ DISHES
1/2	LB BUTTER
1/2	CUP SUGAR
3	PAPAYAS (NOT TOO RIPE; MASHED)
3	OZ GRAND MARNIER
2	T CORN STARCH
12	EGG WHITES (ROOM TEMPERATURE)
	PINCH OF SALT
1/2	CUP POWDERED SUGAR

1. COAT SOUFFLÉ DISHES WITH BUTTER AND DUST WITH SUGAR.
2. IN A MEDIUM SAUCE PAN OVER MEDIUM HEAT, BROWN BUTTER. ADD SUGAR AND CARMELIZE.
3. ADD FRUIT AND GRAND MARNIER. FLAME TO BURN-OFF ALCOHOL.
4. COMBINE CORN STARCH WITH ENOUGH WATER TO MAKE A PASTE. ADD SLOWLY TO THICKEN SAUCE. REMOVE FROM HEAT. SET ASIDE.
5. PRE-HEAT OVEN TO 400 DEGREES.
6. BEAT EGG WHITES UNTIL STIFF, SLOWLY ADDING SALT AND SUGAR.
7. FOLD THREE-FOURTHS OF FRUIT MIXTURE INTO EGG WHITES.
8. DIVIDE MIXTURE EVENLY AMONGST SOUFFLÉ DISHES.
9. PLACE DISHES ON CENTER OF RACK IN PRE-HEATED OVEN AND BAKE 20 MINUTES, UNTIL GOLDEN BROWN.
10. REMOVE FROM OVEN. DUST LIGHTLY WITH POWDERED SUGAR AND SERVE IMMEDIATELY, WITH REMAINDER OF SAUCE ON THE SIDE.

PREPARATION: 30-40 MINUTES
COOKING/BAKING: 15/20 MINUTES
SERVES: 6

KA HONU
GIFT GALLERY

WHALER'S VILLAGE
KAANAPALI BEACH
LAHAINA, MAUI,
HAWAII 96761

FULFILLS YOUR EXPECTATIONS ABOUT FINDING
THAT SPECIAL HAWAIIAN SHOP FOR YOUR GIFT
GIVING NEEDS.

THERE ARE HANDMADE TREASURES TO DELIGHT
EVERY LOVED ONE (INCLUDING YOURSELF, OF
COURSE).

OUR HAWAIIAN CHRISTMAS ORNAMENTS ARE ON
SALE THE YEAR ROUND; THEY'RE SO VERY GIVE-
ABLE AND CERTAINLY COLLECTIBLE.

EXPLORE AMONG HANDMADE
DOLLS AND TOYS, LOVELY ISLAND
CERAMICS AND WINDCHIMES,
COLLECTOR QUALITY BOWLS OF
RARE HAWAIIAN WOODS. A UNIQUE
HANDHELD HARP CRAFTED ON
MAUI OF BEAUTIFUL KOA WOOD,
NEEDLEPOINT KITS OF FAVORITE
FLOWERS, NIIHAU SHELL LEIS AND
MORE – MUCH MORE.

open 9 to 9 every day
call us at 808-661-0173
write for our new brochure

KAANAPALI BEACH HOTEL

TIKI TERRACE

BREAKFAST 7-11 MONDAY-FRIDAY
DINNER 6-9:30 DAILY
CHAMPAGNE BRUNCH 9AM-2PM SUNDAY
RESERVATIONS
661-0011

LOCATED IN THE KAANAPALI BEACH HOTEL
KAANAPALI

TIKI TERRACE

MARINATED MAHI MAHI

THIS DISH IS PREPARED ONE OR TWO DAYS BEFORE SERVING. IT HAS THE ADVANTAGE OF BEING COMPLETELY READY-TO-SERVE AT THE TIME OF THE MEAL.

1   LB. MAHI MAHI (SUB: WHITE FISH)

MARINADE

1/2   CUP CRANBERRY OR CIDER VINEGAR
1   CUP SALAD OIL
1/2   CUP GREEN PEPPER (DICED)
1/2   CUP SHALLOTS (CHOPPED)
1/4   CUP PARSLEY (FRESHLY CHOPPED)
SALT AND PEPPER (TO TASTE)

1. CUT FISH INTO THIN FOUR-OUNCE SLICES.
2. DREDGE FILETS IN FLOUR.
3. IN A LARGE SKILLET, OVER MEDIUM HEAT, IN HOT OIL, BROWN THE FILETS. (DO NOT OVER COOK.)
4. COOL. POUR MARINADE OVER FILETS AND KEEP REFRIGERATED UNTIL READY TO SERVE (AT LEAST 24 HOURS).

PREPARATION: 20-25 MINUTES
COOKING: 15 MINUTES
SERVES: 4-6

TIKI TERRACE

BREAST OF CHICKEN LAHAINA
(MARINATE OVERNIGHT)

1   CHICKEN BREAST (DEBONED)

MARINADE:

1/2   CUP DRY WHITE WINE
1/8   t DRY MARJORAM
1/8   t DRY THYME
1/2   BAY LEAF
1   GARLIC CLOVE (CRUSHED)
SALT (TO TASTE)
PEPPER (TO TASTE)
WORCESTERSHIRE SAUCE (TO TASTE)

1. REMOVE SKIN FROM CHICKEN. POUND CHICKEN BREAST BETWEEN TWO SHEETS OF ALUMINUM FOIL.
2. MARINATE OVERNIGHT IN REFRIGERATOR.
3. COOKING METHOD: GRILL, BROIL OR BARBEQUE.
4. SERVE WITH RICE AND GARNISH WITH FRESH (HAWAIIAN) PINEAPPLE.

PREPARATION: 15 MINUTES
COOKING: 7 MINUTES
SERVES: ONE

SHERATON MAUI

Discovery Room

CONTINENTAL AND AMERICAN CUISINE
BREAKFAST DAILY 6:30-11
DINNER FROM 6:30
RESERVATIONS
661-0031

LOCATED IN THE SHERATON MAUI
KAANAPALI

PICCATA MILANAISE

1   LB PASTA
12 PIECES VEAL (THINLY SLICED)
SALT AND PEPPER (TO TASTE)
1   CUP FLOUR
4   EGGS
1/2 CUP PARMESAN CHEESE (GRATED)
1/2 CUP CLARIFIED BUTTER
1   CUP TOMATO SAUCE
PARMESAN CHEESE (GARNISH)

1. COOK PASTA AL DENTE.
2. SEASON VEAL WITH SALT AND PEPPER. DREDGE IN FLOUR.
3. BEAT EGGS AND MIX IN CHEESE.
4. DIP VEAL IN EGG MIXTURE AND SAUTÉ IN A LARGE SKILLET WITH MELTED BUTTER 3-5 MINUTES ON EACH SIDE. REMOVE FROM PAN AND SET ASIDE. KEEP WARM.
5. IN SAME SKILLET SAUTÉ PASTA (ADD MORE BUTTER, IF NECESSARY) FOR 2-3 MINUTES.
6. ADD TOMATO SAUCE AND COOK TILL SAUCE IS HEATED.
7. PLACE PASTA ON SERVING PLATTER. SERVE WITH VEAL ON TOP.
8. GARNISH WITH PARMESAN CHEESE.

PREPARATION: 20 MINUTES
COOKING: 15-20 MINUTES
SERVES: 6

COUPE HAWAIIAN

6	CHAMPAGNE GLASSES
6	SEPARATE SCOOPS WATERMELON SHERBET
1/3	CUP FRESH PINEAPPLE (DICED)
1/3	CUP FRESH PAPAYA (DICED)
1/3	CUP FRESH APPLE (DICED)
3	T APRICOT MARMALADE
1	T DARK RUM
1	t MACADAMIA NUTS (CHOPPED)
1/2	CUP WHIPPING CREAM (WHIPPED)
1/2	CUP CHOCOLATE SHAVINGS

1. PLACE ONE SMALL SCOOP OF WATERMELON SHERBET IN EACH CHAMPAGNE GLASS AND PLACE IN FREEZER.

2. IN A MIXING BOWL MIX DICED FRUITS, MARMALADE, RUM AND NUTS. LET STAND IN REFRIGERATOR UNTIL READY TO USE.

3. WHEN READY TO SERVE, POUR 2 T. OF FRUIT MIXTURE OVER EACH SCOOP OF SHERBET.

4. DECORATE BY PIPING A ROSETTE OF WHIPPED CREAM OVER THE TOP AND SPRINKLE WITH CHOCOLATE SHAVINGS.

5. SERVE IMMEDIATELY OR HOLD IN FREEZER (NO LONGER THAN 20 MINUTES).

PREPARATION: 20-25 MINUTES
SERVES: 6

BLACK ROCK

CONTINENTAL CUISINE

BREAKFAST 6:30-11

LUNCH 11:30-2:30

DINNER 6-9:30

661-0031

LOCATED IN THE SHERATON MAUI

KAANAPALI

MAHIMAHI THE ISLAND WAY

BLACK ROCK TERRACE

4   SEVEN-OZ MAHIMAHI FILETS
SALT AND PEPPER (TO TASTE)
JUICE OF ONE-HALF LEMON
1   T WORCESTERSHIRE SAUCE
1   CUP FLOUR
4   EGGS
1/2   CUP CLARIFIED BUTTER
2   OZ. MACADAMIA NUTS (CHOPPED)
1/2   LEMON

1. SEASON MAHIMAHI WITH SALT, PEPPER, LEMON JUICE AND WORCESTERSHIRE SAUCE.
   SAUCE.
2. DIP MAHIMAHI IN FLOUR.
3. DIP COATED MAHIMAHI INTO BEATEN EGGS.
4. HEAT HALF OF THE CLARIFIED BUTTER IN FRYING PAN. FRY FISH FILETS TO A
   GOLDEN BROWN.
5. REMOVE FILETS. PLACE ON SERVING DISH.
6. SPRINKLE MAHIMAHI WITH MACADAMIA NUTS.
7. SQUEEZE THE LEMON-HALF INTO REMAINING BUTTER. POUR BUTTER OVER FISH.
8. SERVE IMMEDIATELY WITH RICE AND FRESH VEGETABLES.

PREPARATION: 15-20 MINUTES
COOKING: 15-20 MINUTES
SERVES: 4

BLACK ROCK TERRACE

PEACHES IN BRANDY CREAM

6   EGGS (SEPARATED)
1|2   CUP SUGAR
1|2   CUP BRANDY
1|2   CUP WHIPPING CREAM
1|3   CUP SHREDDED COCONUT (OVEN BROWNED)
12   CANNED PEACH HALVES (NO JUICE)

1. WHIP EGG YOLKS AND SUGAR IN ELECTRIC BLENDER UNTIL THICK AND FLUFFY.
2. REDUCE SPEED AND GRADUALLY ADD BRANDY.
3. WHIP WHIPPING CREAM UNTIL STIFF; FOLD INTO EGG YOLK MIXTURE.
4. BEAT EGG WHITES UNTIL STIFF; FOLD CAREFULLY INTO EGG YOLK AND CREAM MIXTURE.
5. PLACE TWO PEACH HALVES INTO EACH OF SIX SMALL GLASS BOWLS.
6. POUR THE BRANDY CREAM OVER THE PEACHES. SPRINKLE WITH BROWNED SHREDDED COCONUT. SERVE.

PREPARATION: 15-20 MINUTES
BROWNING OF COCONUT: 3-5 MINUTES
SERVES: 6

The Peacock
RESTAURANT

POLYNESIAN CUISINE AND SEAFOOD

DINNER SERVED FROM 6 PM EVERY EVENING

RESERVATIONS

667-6847

2650 KEKAA DRIVE

KAANAPALI

The Peacock

CRAB AND MUSHROOM
STUFFED ARTICHOKE HEARTS

4   OZ. MUSHROOMS (SLICED)
1   12-OZ. CAN CRAB MEAT
1/2   MEDIUM ONION (DICED FINE)
2   EGGS
3/4   CUP PANKO FLAKES (FLOUR BREADING MEAL)
1/4   t BLACK PEPPER
PINCH OF SALT
1/2   t SEASONED SALT
DASH OF TABASCO SAUCE
2   7-OZ. CANS ARTICHOKE HEARTS
MORNEY SAUCE (NEXT RECIPE)
1/4   CUP SWISS CHEESE (SPRINKLE)

1. BOIL MUSHROOMS UNTIL TENDER, 15-20 MINUTES.
2. WHILE BOILING MUSHROOMS, PREPARE MORNEY SAUCE (NEXT RECIPE).
3. DRAIN MUSHROOMS AND RUN THEM THROUGH COARSE SETTING ON BLENDER.
4. IN A LARGE MIXING BOWL MIX TOGETHER CRAB MEAT, ONIONS, EGGS, PANKO
   FLAKES AND SEASONINGS. SET ASIDE.
5. PREHEAT OVEN TO 400 DEGREES.
6. DRAIN CANNED ARTICHOKE HEARTS. CUT STEMS TO LIE FLAT ON BAKING DISH.
7. PLACE ICE CREAM SCOOP OF STUFFING MIXTURE INTO EACH ARTICHOKE HEART.
8. PLACE IN OVEN FOR 5 MINUTES.

continued

The Peacock

9. REMOVE FROM OVEN. LADLE MORNEY SAUCE OVER THE STUFFED ARTICHOKES. SPRINKLE WITH SWISS CHEESE. RETURN TO OVEN FOR TWO MINUTES.

10. SERVE IMMEDIATELY, WITH SLICED FRENCH BREAD.

PREPARATION: 15-20 MINUTES
COOKING/BAKING: 20 MINUTES / 7-10 MINUTES
SERVES: 8

MORNEY SAUCE

1-1/2	CUPS MILK
4	OZ BUTTER
2	T FLOUR
1/2	CUP SWISS CHEESE (GRATED)
1/4	t SALT
1/2	t WHITE PEPPER
1	t NUTMEG

1. IN A SAUCEPAN HEAT MILK TO BOILING.
2. IN ANOTHER PAN MAKE A ROUX BY MELTING BUTTER AND ADDING FLOUR. STIR CONSTANTLY.
3. ADD CHEESE AND SEASONINGS. KEEP WARM.

PREPARATION: 2-3 MINUTES
COOKING: 5 MINUTES
YIELDS: 2 CUPS

THE ROYAL LAHAINA RESORT

THE ROYAL LAHAINA IS A COMPLETE RESORT WITH A WIDE VARIETY OF ACCOMODATIONS, FACILITIES AND ACTIVITIES, ONE OF THE TEN HOTEL-RESORTS IN HAWAII OPERATED BY AMFAC HOTELS. THE ROYAL LAHAINA'S 704 ROOMS, FROM THE BEACH AND GARDEN COTTAGES TO THE 12-STORY LAHAINA KAI TOWER, ARE SURROUNDED BY 52 ACRES OF TROPICAL GARDEN! THE ROYAL LAHAINA IS MAUI'S VENERABLE RESORT, HAVING BEEN THE FIRST KAANAPALI RESORT TO HAVE OPENED ITS DOORS (1963). IT IS CERTAINLY ONE OF MAUI'S FINEST RESORTS, WITH A CHARACTER AND CHARM ONLY TIME AND EXPERIENCE CAN CREATE. THE ROYAL LAHAINA OFFERS FULL SERVICES TO ITS GUESTS INCLUDING RETAIL AND SUNDRY SHOPS, DRY-CLEANING AND CAR RENTAL SERVICES AND EVEN MASSAGES (BY APPOINTMENT)!

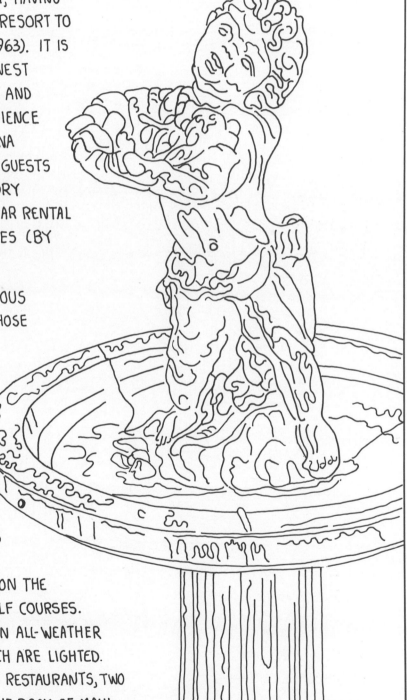

THE RESORT FRONTS ON FAMOUS KAANAPALI BEACH ITSELF-WHOSE BEAUTIFUL WHITE SANDS STRETCH FOR THREE MILES. RESORT ACTIVITIES ARE EXTENSIVE, INCLUDING SAILING, SNORKELING, DIVING, WIND SURFING AND SWIMMING-IN THE WARM PACIFIC OR IN THE SIX RESORT POOLS! GOLFERS WILL ENJOY THE 36 HOLES OF CHAMPIONSHIP GOLF NEARBY ON THE FAMOUS ROYAL KAANAPALI GOLF COURSES. TENNIS PLAYERS WILL FIND TEN ALL-WEATHER PLEXIPAVE COURTS, SIX OF WHICH ARE LIGHTED. THE ROYAL LAHAINA HAS FINE RESTAURANTS, TWO OF WHICH ARE FEATURED IN THE BOOK OF MAUI.

THE ROYAL LAHAINA RESORT

THE Royal Lahaina RESORT

MAUI'S ORIGINAL PREMIERE RESORT, AT THE HEART OF KAANAPALI

Guest rooms, restaurants and amenities to please every taste. Modern high rise suites and deluxe accommodations, spacious, quiet and rambling cottages with garden, golf course and ocean views. All located just steps from Hawaii's finest golden sand beach.

Restaurants to delight every palate...Don the Beachcomber's famous polynesian and cantonese cuisine, seafood specialties at popular Moby Dick's, nightly Luaus at sunset, right on the beach with spectacular fireworks display for the grand finale.

Top flight entertainment in the Alii Show Room and whale watching breakfasts on the Ocean Terrace or the piece d'resistance...Royal Lahaina's famous Sunday Champagne Brunch.

All yours to savor...to enjoy...to experience at the Royal Lahaina Resort.

Moby Dick's   Disco Dancing   Don the Beachcomber   Sunday Champagne Brunch

Give us a call...(808) 661-3611

THE Royal Lahaina RESORT
KAANAPALI, MAUI
Amfac Hotels

Moby Dick's

SEAFOOD
DINNER NIGHTLY
6-9:30 PM
RESERVATION
661-3611

LOCATED IN THE
ROYAL LAHAINA RESORT
KAANAPALI

Moby Dick's

MOBY DICK'S BOUILLABAISE
(MARINATE OVERNIGHT)

1/4	LB OPAKAPAKA
1/4	LB ONO
6	OZ SCALLOPS
8	PIECES MAUI PRAWNS
1	LB MAUI LOBSTER
8	CLAMS
8	MUSSELS
1	CUP OLIVE OIL
1/4	CUP PERNOD
1	t FRESH FENNEL
2	T PARSLEY
1/2	LB FRESH FISH BONES

LOBSTER SHELLS

SHRIMP SHELLS

1	LEAK (CHOPPED)
1	CELERY STICK (CHOPPED)
1	ONION (CHOPPED)
1	t WHITE PEPPERCORNS
1	BAY LEAF
1	CLOVE OF GARLIC (MINCED)
1	CUP WHITE WINE
1/4	CUP OLIVE OIL
1	LEEK (JULIENNE)
1/4	CUP FRESH FENNEL (JULIENNE)
1/2	CUP CARROTS (JULIENNE)

Continued...

Moby Dick's

(CONTINUED)
1/2 CUP CELERY (JULIENNE)
1 CLOVE OF GARLIC (MINCED)
4 TOMATOES
PINCH OF SAFFRON
PINCH OF WHITE PEPPER
1/4 CUP PERNOD
2 CUPS CHABLIS
1/4 CUP OLIVE OIL
2 T SHALLOTS (CHOPPED)
FENNEL (CHOPPED, GARNISH)
DILL WEED (CHOPPED, GARNISH)

1. IN A LARGE CASSEROLE DISH PLACE FISH IN OIL, PERNOD, FENNEL AND PARSLEY. PLACE IN REFRIGERATOR TO MARINATE OVERNIGHT.
2. IN A LARGE POT COVER FISH BONES, LOBSTER SHELLS AND SHRIMP SHELLS WITH 6 CUPS WATER AND BRING TO A BOIL. ADD LEEK, CELERY, ONION, SEASONINGS AND WINE. SIMMER 35 MINUTES. STRAIN, RESERVING 3 CUPS LIQUID. SET ASIDE.
3. IN A LARGE SOUP POT, WITH HOT OIL, SAUTE JULIENNE VEGETABLES AND GARLIC 5 MIN.
4. ADD TOMATOES, SAFFRON, PEPPER, PERNOD, AND CHABLIS. REDUCE ONE-HALF (15 MIN.).
5. IN A LARGE SKILLET, HEAT OIL AND COOK PRAWNS AND LOBSTER UNTIL RED. ADD FISH AND SAUTÉ 3-5 MINUTES EACH SIDE.
6. ADD SHALLOTS, CLAMS AND MUSSELS. COOK 10 MINUTES.
7. PLACE COOKED FISH IN SOUP POT. ADD FISH STOCK AND SIMMER 5 MINUTES.
8. POUR INTO INDIVIDUAL SOUP BOWLS. SPRINKLE WITH FENNEL LEAVES, DILL.
9. SERVE WITH HOT GARLIC BREAD.

PREPARATION: 25-30 MINUTES
COOKING: 1 HOUR 25 MINUTES (DOESN'T INCLUDE MARINATING TIME)
SERVES: 4

THE ROYAL LAHAINA RESORT

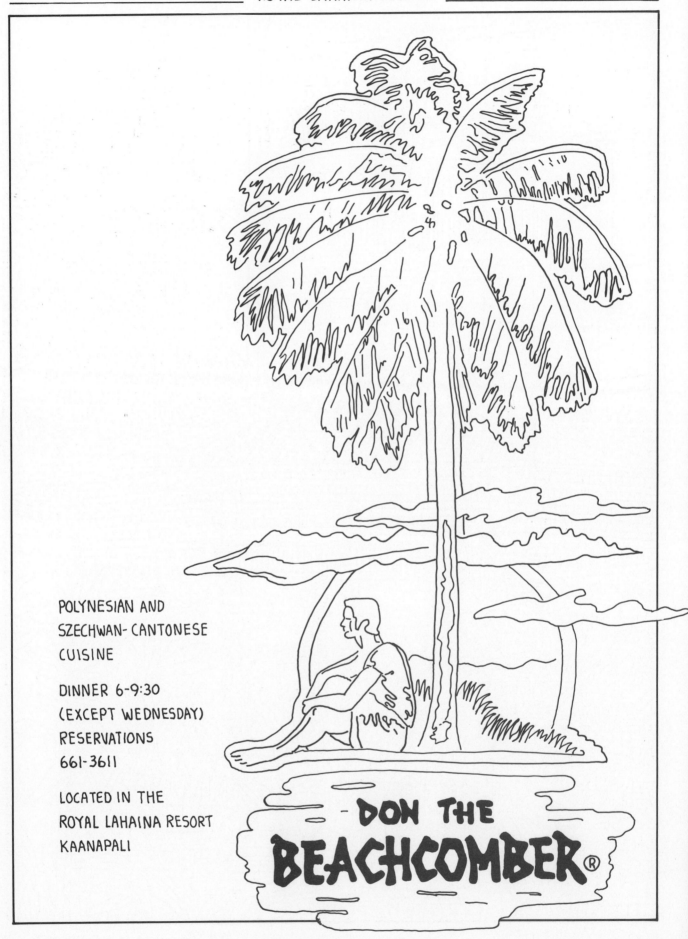

POLYNESIAN AND
SZECHWAN-CANTONESE
CUISINE

DINNER 6-9:30
(EXCEPT WEDNESDAY)
RESERVATIONS
661-3611

LOCATED IN THE
ROYAL LAHAINA RESORT
KAANAPALI

DON THE BEACHCOMBER®

SOO SUI GAI

1   CUP CHICKEN (COOKED, SHREDDED)
1   T GREEN ONION
1   t SESAME SEEDS
3   DROPS SESAME OIL
1   T CHINESE CATSUP
1   T CHINESE HOT MUSTARD
2   T PEANUTS (CHOPPED)
1   CUP RICE NOODLES (COOKED)
1   t RED GINGER
1   CUP LETTUCE (CHOPPED)
1   T SALAD OIL

TOSS ALL INGREDIENTS IN LARGE BOWL.

PREPARATION: 25-30 MINUTES
(CHICKEN COOKING TIME NOT INCLUDED)
SERVES: 4

DON THE BEACHCOMBER®

SZECHUAN PEPPER FILET
(MARINATE AT LEAST 4 HRS)

1/2	LB	FLANK STEAK
2	OZ	SOY SAUCE
2	OZ	OIL
		PINCH OF BAKING SODA
3	T	OIL
2	T	GINGER (SHREDDED)
2		CLOVES GARLIC (MINCED)
1	t	SZECHUAN HOT BEAN SAUCE
1		SMALL GREEN PEPPER (JULIENNE)
2	OZ	BAMBOO SHOOTS (JULIENNE)
1	t	SUGAR
1		LARGE LEEK (JULIENNE)
2		SCALLIONS (JULIENNE)

CORNSTARCH (MIXED WITH WATER)

1. CUT STEAK INTO ONE INCH STRIPS. MARINATE IN SOY SAUCE, OIL AND BAKING SODA. (MARINATE IN REFRIGERATOR.)
2. IN A MEDIUM WOK HEAT OIL.
3. ADD GINGER, GARLIC AND BEAN SAUCE. STIR-FRY OVER MEDIUM HEAT 2-3 MINUTES.
4. ADD STEAK AND STIR-FRY UNTIL DONE (ABOUT 7 MINUTES).
5. ADD ALL REMAINING INGREDIENTS EXCEPT THE CORNSTARCH AND WATER MIXTURE.
6. THICKEN SAUCE WITH CORNSTARCH MIXTURE.
7. SERVE OVER RICE OR NOODLES.

PREPARATION: 15-20 MINUTES
(DOES NOT INCLUDE MARINATING TIME)
COOKING: 12-15 MINUTES
SERVES: 2

TO NAPILI-KAPALUA

30

UNDER
CONSTRUCTION

ALAELOA BEACH

KAHANA

COASTAL HIGHWAY

MAHINAHINA

HONOKOWAI BEACH PARK

HONOKOWAI

HONOAPIILANI
HIGHWAY (30)

HONOKOWAI POINT

KAANAPALI
AIRPORT

60'   18'

TO KAANAPALI

THIS AREA OF MAUI COULD BE OVERLOOKED AS YOU DRIVE ALONG THE NEW HONOAPIILANI HIGHWAY BETWEEN KAANAPALI BEACH RESORT AND KAPALUA RESORT, SO UNLESS YOU ARE IN A RUSH TAKE THE OLD COASTAL HIGHWAY. AND IF YOU are IN A RUSH, PLEASE SLOW DOWN A LITTLE SO THAT YOU WILL feel MAUI AS WELL AS SEE IT!

HONOKOWAI BEACH PARK IS A FULL FACILITY PARK WITH RESTROOMS, SHOWERS, TABLES, ETC. THE SAND BEACH IS NOT LARGE BUT IT IS VERY SAFE. IT HAS A NATURAL SAND-BOTTOMED POOL WHICH IS PERFECT FOR CHILDREN TO PLAY IN. SWIMMING AND SNORKELING ARE FAIR.

KAHANA BEACH IS A LONG, CURVING, WHITE SAND BEACH. KAHANA WAS ONCE A LITTLE PLANTATION TOWN BUT MOST LOCAL HOUSING HERE (AND FROM HONOKOWAI TO KAPALUA AS WELL) HAS BEEN TORN DOWN TO MAKE ROOM FOR THE MANY NEW RESORTS. THIS IS AN AREA OF CONDO-HOTEL COMPLEXES SUCH AS HOTEL CORPORATION OF THE PACIFIC'S KAANAPALI SHORES HOTEL AND THE CONDOMINIUM COMPLEXES OF MAHANA AND SANDS OF KAHANA. THE SUNSHINE IS CONSTANT HERE BUT NOT AS RELENTLESS AS IN LAHAINA. THE VIEW FROM THE WHITE SAND BEACHES IS MOST ELEGANT: LANAI, MOLOKAI, THE SETTING SUN AND LEAPING HUMPBACK WHALES! MANY OF THE RESORTS HERE ARE FULL SERVICE AND WITH EASY ACCESS TO NAPILI-KAPALUA AND KAANAPALI-LAHAINA, THIS IS A VERY CONVENIENT VACATION AREA!

HONOKOWAI TO KAHANA

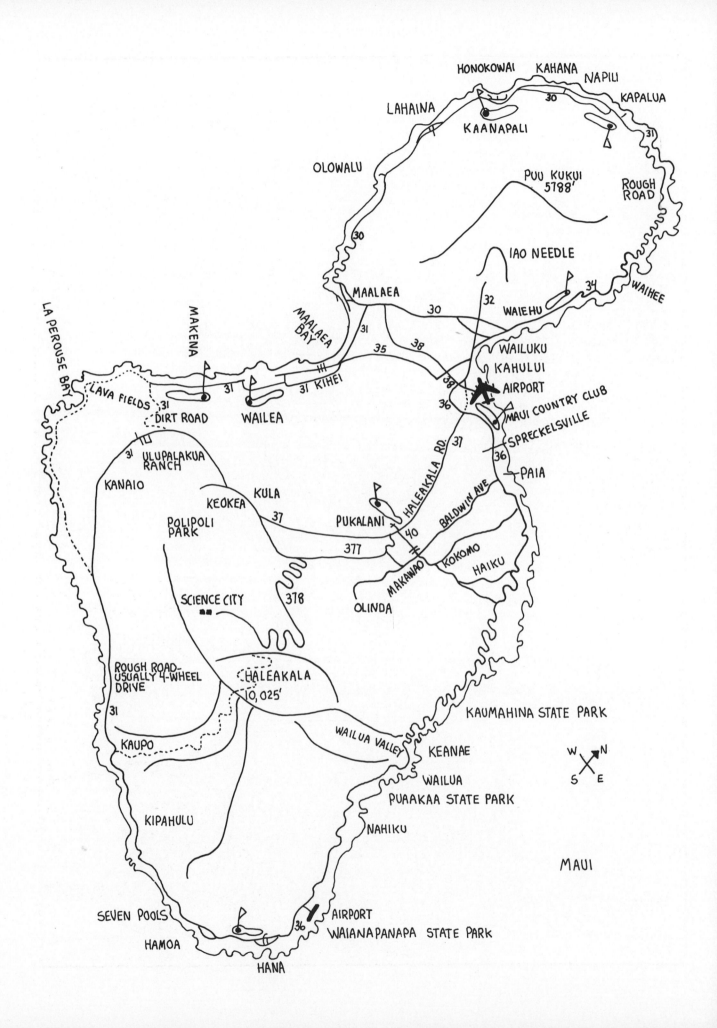

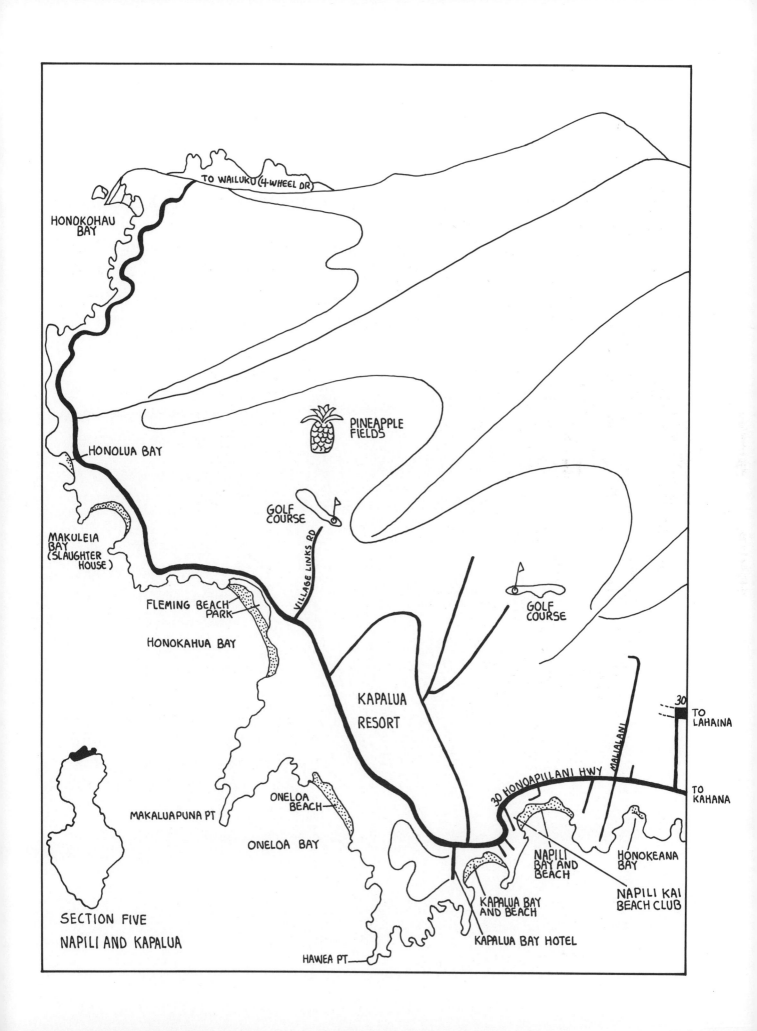

TO WAILUKU (4-WHEEL DR)

HONOKOHAU
BAY

HONOLUA BAY

PINEAPPLE
FIELDS

GOLF
COURSE

MAKULEIA
BAY
(SLAUGHTER
HOUSE)

VILLAGE LINKS RD

GOLF
COURSE

FLEMING BEACH
PARK

HONOKAHUA BAY

KAPALUA
RESORT

30
TO
LAHAINA

MALIALANI

30 HONOAPIILANI HWY

TO
KAHANA

MAKALUAPUNA PT

ONELOA
BEACH

NAPILI
BAY AND
BEACH

HONOKEANA
BAY

ONELOA BAY

KAPALUA BAY
AND BEACH

NAPILI KAI
BEACH CLUB

SECTION FIVE
NAPILI AND KAPALUA

KAPALUA BAY HOTEL

HAWEA PT

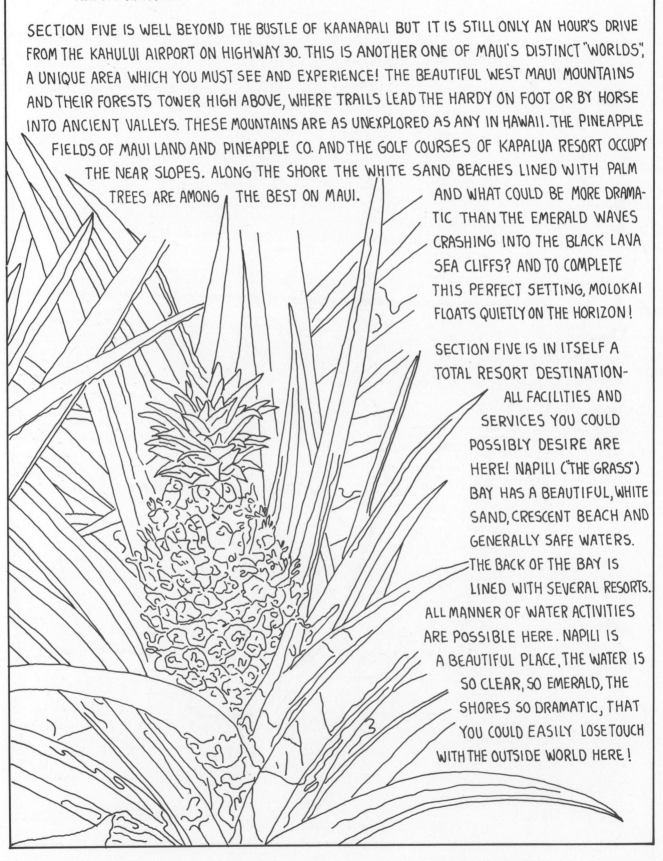

SECTION FIVE

NAPILI-KAPALUA

SECTION FIVE IS WELL BEYOND THE BUSTLE OF KAANAPALI BUT IT IS STILL ONLY AN HOUR'S DRIVE FROM THE KAHULUI AIRPORT ON HIGHWAY 30. THIS IS ANOTHER ONE OF MAUI'S DISTINCT "WORLDS", A UNIQUE AREA WHICH YOU MUST SEE AND EXPERIENCE! THE BEAUTIFUL WEST MAUI MOUNTAINS AND THEIR FORESTS TOWER HIGH ABOVE, WHERE TRAILS LEAD THE HARDY ON FOOT OR BY HORSE INTO ANCIENT VALLEYS. THESE MOUNTAINS ARE AS UNEXPLORED AS ANY IN HAWAII. THE PINEAPPLE FIELDS OF MAUI LAND AND PINEAPPLE CO. AND THE GOLF COURSES OF KAPALUA RESORT OCCUPY THE NEAR SLOPES. ALONG THE SHORE THE WHITE SAND BEACHES LINED WITH PALM TREES ARE AMONG THE BEST ON MAUI.

AND WHAT COULD BE MORE DRAMATIC THAN THE EMERALD WAVES CRASHING INTO THE BLACK LAVA SEA CLIFFS? AND TO COMPLETE THIS PERFECT SETTING, MOLOKAI FLOATS QUIETLY ON THE HORIZON!

SECTION FIVE IS IN ITSELF A TOTAL RESORT DESTINATION- ALL FACILITIES AND SERVICES YOU COULD POSSIBLY DESIRE ARE HERE! NAPILI ("THE GRASS") BAY HAS A BEAUTIFUL, WHITE SAND, CRESCENT BEACH AND GENERALLY SAFE WATERS. THE BACK OF THE BAY IS LINED WITH SEVERAL RESORTS. ALL MANNER OF WATER ACTIVITIES ARE POSSIBLE HERE. NAPILI IS A BEAUTIFUL PLACE. THE WATER IS SO CLEAR, SO EMERALD, THE SHORES SO DRAMATIC, THAT YOU COULD EASILY LOSE TOUCH WITH THE OUTSIDE WORLD HERE!

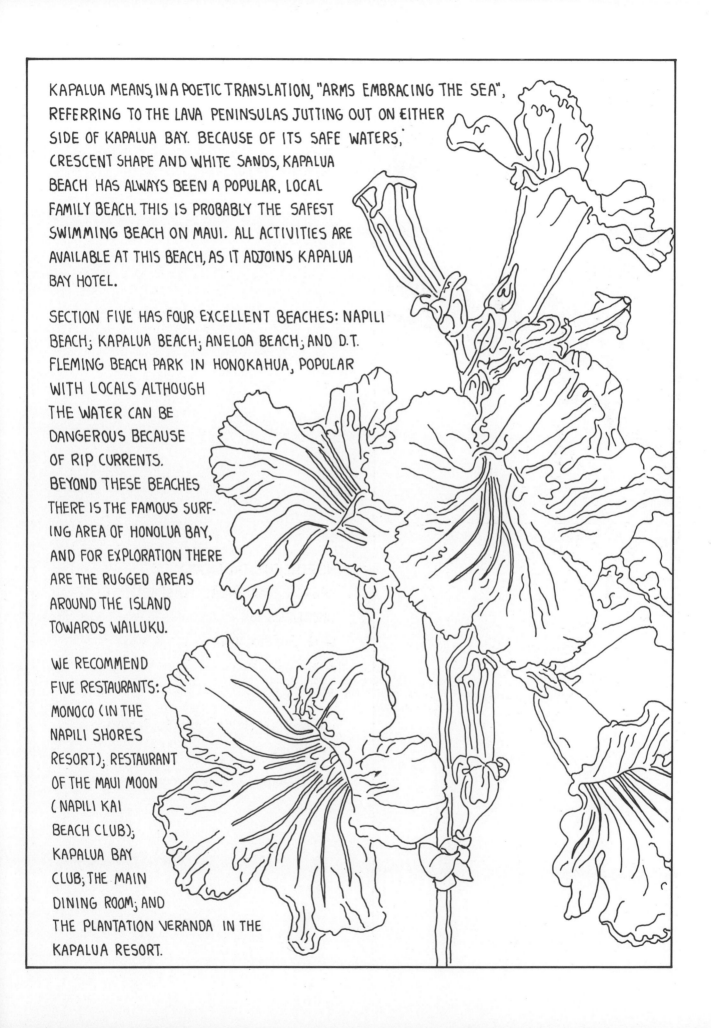

KAPALUA MEANS, IN A POETIC TRANSLATION, "ARMS EMBRACING THE SEA",
REFERRING TO THE LAVA PENINSULAS JUTTING OUT ON EITHER
SIDE OF KAPALUA BAY. BECAUSE OF ITS SAFE WATERS,
CRESCENT SHAPE AND WHITE SANDS, KAPALUA
BEACH HAS ALWAYS BEEN A POPULAR, LOCAL
FAMILY BEACH. THIS IS PROBABLY THE SAFEST
SWIMMING BEACH ON MAUI. ALL ACTIVITIES ARE
AVAILABLE AT THIS BEACH, AS IT ADJOINS KAPALUA
BAY HOTEL.

SECTION FIVE HAS FOUR EXCELLENT BEACHES: NAPILI
BEACH; KAPALUA BEACH; ANELOA BEACH; AND D.T.
FLEMING BEACH PARK IN HONOKAHUA, POPULAR
WITH LOCALS ALTHOUGH
THE WATER CAN BE
DANGEROUS BECAUSE
OF RIP CURRENTS.
BEYOND THESE BEACHES
THERE IS THE FAMOUS SURF-
ING AREA OF HONOLUA BAY,
AND FOR EXPLORATION THERE
ARE THE RUGGED AREAS
AROUND THE ISLAND
TOWARDS WAILUKU.

WE RECOMMEND
FIVE RESTAURANTS:
MONOCO (IN THE
NAPILI SHORES
RESORT); RESTAURANT
OF THE MAUI MOON
(NAPILI KAI
BEACH CLUB);
KAPALUA BAY
CLUB; THE MAIN
DINING ROOM; AND
THE PLANTATION VERANDA IN THE
KAPALUA RESORT.

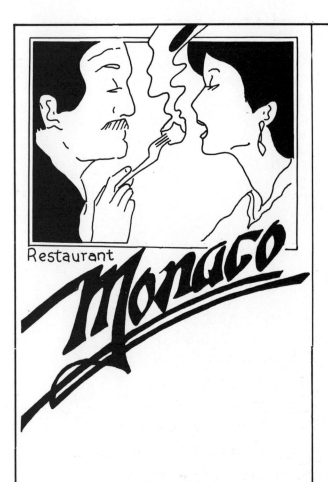

Restaurant Monaco

NORTHERN ITALIAN AND
FRENCH PROVENCAL CUISINE
DINNER 6-10
LATE SUPPER 10-12
RESERVATIONS
669-8077

LOCATED IN NAPILI SHORES RESORT
NAPILI

SHRIMP SCAMPI

1	LB FRESH PRAWNS
1/4	CUP OLIVE OIL
2	OZ PERNOD
1/2	CUP CHICKEN STOCK
2	OZ WHITE WINE
2	CLOVES GARLIC (MINCED)
2	OZ BUTTER

SALT AND PEPPER (TO TASTE)
JUICE OF ONE LEMON

1. CLEAN, PEEL AND DEVEIN SHRIMP
2. IN A LARGE SKILLET, WITH HOT OIL, SAUTÉ SHRIMP UNTIL NEARLY PINK (ONE MINUTE ON EACH SIDE).
3. POUR PERNOD OVER SHRIMP AND IGNITE. WAIT FOR FLAME TO FADE.
4. ADD CHICKEN STOCK, WINE AND GARLIC. COOK FIVE MINUTES.
5. THICKEN WITH BUTTER. ADD SALT, PEPPER AND LEMON JUICE.
6. SERVE WITH WILD RICE AND FRESH VEGETABLES.

PREPARATION: 15-20 MINUTES
COOKING: 7-10 MINUTES
SERVES: 4

KAHLUA CHEESE CAKE
(REFRIGERATE 3 HOURS)

18	OZ CREAM CHEESE
2|3	CUP SUGAR
1|3	CUP KAHLUA
2	EGGS
1	GRAHAM CRACKER PIE SHELL
1|4	CUP SUGAR
1	CUP SOUR CREAM

1. PREHEAT OVEN TO 365 DEGREES.
2. IN A BLENDER MIX TOGETHER CREAM CHEESE, SUGAR AND KAHLUA FOR 3 MINUTES (HIGH SPEED).
3. ADD EGGS ONE AT A TIME, BLENDING UNTIL SMOOTH.
4. POUR INTO PIE CRUST. BAKE IN LOWER THIRD OF OVEN FOR 20 MINUTES. CHEESE CAKE SHOULD NOT BE COMPLETELY SET.
5. REMOVE FROM OVEN. COOL ONE HOUR TO ROOM TEMPERATURE. PLACE IN REFRIGERATOR FOR ONE HOUR.
6. MIX TOGETHER SOUR CREAM AND SUGAR. SPREAD OVER CAKE. REFRIGERATE TWO MORE HOURS.

PREPARATION: 10 MINUTES
COOKING: 20 MINUTES
SERVES: 10

NAPILI KAI BEACH CLUB

NAPILI KAI BEACH CLUB

NAPILI KAI BEACH CLUB IS A LOW RISE OASIS ON NAPILI BAY. IT IS ONE OF THE OLDEST RESORTS ON MAUI (CONSTRUCTION BEGAN IN 1960). WHAT WAS NAPILI LIKE BACK THEN, AT THE VERY BEGINNING OF MAUI'S RESORT DAYS, BEFORE THE DEVELOPMENT OF KAANAPALI, KAPALUA, KAHANA, KIHEI AND WAILEA? JACK MILLAR, CLUB DIRECTOR, WROTE: "THE BAY IN SUMMER IS EVEN MORE BEAUTIFUL THAN IN WINTER, THE CLIMATE DRIER THAN HONOLULU AND MUCH MORE PLEASANT. SLEEPING EACH NIGHT WAS A THRILL BECAUSE OF THE CONSTANT BREEZE AND THE DRY AIR WHICH MIXED WITH THE BOOM OF THE SURF SLAPPING ON THE BEACH. IN MY LIFE I HAVE NEVER BEFORE SLEPT UNDER SUCH DELIGHTFUL CIRCUMSTANCES! I BELIEVE OUR LOCATION IS AS BEAUTIFUL AS ANYTHING IN ALL THE ISLANDS."

THE BEAUTY AND CHARM OF NAPILI IS STILL THE SAME BUT THE NAPILI KAI BEACH CLUB HAS GROWN INTO AN EIGHT BUILDING TOTAL ACTIVITY CENTER. THE STAFF HAS GROWN WITH THE NAPILI KAI AND YOU WILL FEEL THE PERSONAL TOUCH WHICH HAS BEEN DEFINED AND REFINED FOR THESE PAST TWENTY YEARS. DURING THE WINTER MONTHS 80 PERCENT OF THE GUESTS ARE REPEAT VISITORS, RETURNING FOR THE UNHURRIED AND SUPERB SERVICE.

THE CLUB INCLUDES A RESTAURANT, (FEATURED IN THIS BOOK), FIVE SWIMMING POOLS, TENNIS COURTS AND MAUI'S LARGEST JACUZZI! NAPILI KAI BEACH CLUB - A PLACE TO ESCAPE FROM THE EVERYDAY LIFE!

"The Unhurried Way of Life"

NAPILI KAI BEACH CLUB

RESTAURANT OF THE MAUI MOON

AMERICAN CUISINE
SEAFOOD

BREAKFAST 8-11
LUNCH 12-3
DINNER 6:30-9:30
SUNDAY BRUNCH 10:30AM-2PM
RESERVATIONS
669-6271

LOCATED ON THE BEACH
AT NAPILI BAY

VEAL FORESTIERE

1   FIVE-OZ. SLICE VEAL
FLOUR (TO DREDGE)
SALT AND PEPPER (TO TASTE)
4   OZ. CLARIFIED BUTTER
2   OZ. MUSHROOMS (SLICED)
1   CLOVE GARLIC (MINCED)
1   OZ. WHITE WINE
2   OZ. HEAVY CREAM

RESTAURANT OF THE MAUI MOON

1. DREDGE VEAL WITH FLOUR AND SEASON WITH SALT AND PEPPER.
2. IN A SMALL SKILLET MELT 2 OZ. OF THE BUTTER AND SAUTÉ VEAL UNTIL GOLDEN BROWN (3-5 MINUTES EACH SIDE).
3. REMOVE VEAL AND PLACE ON SERVING PLATTER. KEEP WARM.
4. IN THE SAME SKILLET MELT REMAINING BUTTER. SAUTÉ MUSHROOMS AND GARLIC (2-3 MINUTES).
5. ADD WINE AND REDUCE ONE-HALF (2-3 MINUTES).
6. ADD CREAM. COOK ONE MINUTE AND SERVE IMMEDIATELY WITH WILD RICE.

PREPARATION: 5 MINUTES
COOKING: 12-15 MINUTES
SERVES: ONE

ARTICHOKE BOTTOM WITH CRABMEAT (APPETIZER)

2   8-OZ CANS ARTICHOKE BOTTOMS
1   LB. CRABMEAT
1   CUP MAYONNAISE
2   LARGE PIMIENTOS (DICED)
3   OZ. BRANDY
JUICE OF ONE LEMON
SALT AND PEPPER (TO TASTE)
1   CUP OF YOUR FAVORITE CHEESE (GRATED)

1. DRAIN ARTICHOKE BOTTOMS AND
   PLACE ON CASSEROLE DISH.
2. IN A LARGE BOWL MIX TOGETHER
   ALL REMAINING INGREDIENTS
   EXCEPT CHEESE.
3. SPOON MIXTURE OVER
   ARTICHOKE BOTTOMS.
4. TOP WITH CHEESE AND
   BAKE AT 350 DEGREES
   UNTIL CHEESE MELTS.

PREPARATION: 20 MINUTES
COOKING: 3-4 MINUTES
SERVES: 8-10

RESTAURANT OF THE MAUI MOON

KAPALUA

KAPALUA BAY HOTEL AND VILLAS

THE KAPALUA BAY HOTEL AND VILLAS ARE THE MOST STRIKING FEATURES OF KAPALUA RESORT.
THIS EXCLUSIVE, TOTALLY PLANNED AND INTEGRATED RESORT COMMUNITY IS A WORLD-CLASS
PRESENTATION OF REGENT INTERNATIONAL HOTELS. ON A STRETCH OF 18 OCEAN-FRONT ACRES,
THE ELEGANT HOTEL FACES LANAI, MOLOKAI AND THE EXQUISITE SETTING SUN! BEYOND THE WHITE
SAND BEACH PROTECTED BY A CORAL REEF AND BORDERED BY A PALM GROVE IS A 750 ACRE RESORT
WHICH ENCOMPASSES A TENNIS GARDEN, TWO ARNOLD PALMER-DESIGNED GOLF COURSES, SWIMMING
POOLS, THREE BEACHES, MANY DELIGHTFUL SHOPS AND THREE EXCELLENT RESTAURANTS!

THIS IS A BEAUTIFUL RESORT, WELL-MANAGED AND REPLETE WITH ALL MANNER OF ISLAND ACTIVITY.
BUT PERHAPS KAPALUA RESORT'S MOST PLEASING FEATURE IS ITS GRACIOUS, HOSPITABLE ATMOSPHERE!

For all the reasons you came to Maui . . .

Kapalua

Only 20 minutes from Lahaina, *Kapalua* is another world. Surrounded by 23,000 acres of unspoiled land this unique resort is a far cry from the busy streets of Waikiki. Three superb restaurants, the sunset luau and weekly wine tasting, two Arnold Palmer championship golf courses, a ten-court Tennis Garden, fine shopping, uncrowded golden sand beaches and, of course, the magnificent Kapalua Bay Hotel and Kapalua Villas.

Dinner Reservations 669-5656   The Tennis Garden 669-5677   The Golf Club 669-8044

The Bay Club

NOUVELLE AND
CONTINENTAL CUISINE
LUNCH 12-2:30
DINNER 6-9:30
RESERVATIONS
669-5656
LOCATED IN KAPALUA RESORT
KAPALUA

The Bay Club

BILLY BI MUSSEL SOUP

6   MUSSELS
2-3 SHALLOTS
1   OZ WHITE WINE
1   BAY LEAF
DASH OF DILL
DASH OF CURRY POWDER
DASH OF SEASONING SALT
1   t PARSLEY (CHOPPED)
SALT AND PEPPER (TO TASTE)
2   OZ HEAVY CREAM
1   STICK CELERY (JULIENNE)
1   CARROT, SMALL (JULIENNE)

1. SIMMER MUSSELS AND SHALLOTS WITH WINE AND SEASONINGS (10 MINUTES).
2. ADD CREAM AND SIMMER FOR FIVE MINUTES. REMOVE FROM HEAT.
3. CORRECT SEASONINGS. ADD JULIENNE OF VEGETABLES.

PREPARATION: 5 MINUTES
COOKING: 20 MINUTES
SERVES: ONE

The Bay Club

FRIED ICE CREAM

1   SPONGE CAKE (CUT IN ONE-FOURTH INCH SLICES)
1   PINT VANILLA ICE CREAM
RASPBERRIES (GARNISH)
BATTER:
3 EGGS
1/4 t VANILLA
2   T SUGAR
1/2 t CORNSTARCH

1. SET A CLOTH ON A TABLE TOP. PLACE ONE SLICE OF CAKE IN THE CENTER.
2. SET ONE SCOOP OF ICE CREAM ON TOP OF THE CAKE. LIFT THE CLOTH UP FROM THE TABLE BY GATHERING THE FOUR CORNERS TOGETHER SIMULTANEOUSLY, GRASPING THE ICE CREAM AND TWISTING IT INTO A BALL. (THE RESULT SHOULD THUS BE A BALL OF ICE CREAM IN A COATING OF CAKE. WRAP THE BALLS INDIVIDUALLY IN ALUMINUM FOIL AND FREEZE FOR AT LEAST TWO HOURS.)
3. PREPARE THE BATTER BY BEATING THE EGGS AND ALL OTHER INGREDIENTS TOGETHER IN A BOWL.
4. REMOVE THE ICE CREAM BALLS FROM THE FREEZER AND DIP THEM INTO THE BATTER.
5. DEEP FRY THEM IN A PREHEATED (375°) FRYER UNTIL A GOLDEN COLOR. (THIS SHOULD TAKE NO LONGER THAN 2 MINUTES.)
6. SET ICE CREAM BALLS ON A DRY CLOTH TO ABSORB EXCESS OIL. SERVE ON A CHILLED PLATE. TOP WITH RASPBERRIES.

PREPARATION: 45 MINUTES
FREEZING/ FRYING: 1 HOUR/ 12 MINUTES
SERVES: 6

KAPALUA BAY HOTEL

Kapalua Bay Hotel

THE DINING ROOM

FRENCH CUISINE
BREAKFAST 7-10
DINNER 6-9:30
RESERVATIONS
669-5656
JACKETS SUGGESTED FOR
GENTLEMEN AT DINNER

Kapalua Bay Hotel

THE MAIN DINING ROOM

BAKED PAPAYA WALTER

3	PAPAYAS, CUT IN HALF AND SEEDED
1-1/2 CUPS	CREAM CHEESE
1-1/2 CUPS	COTTAGE CHEESE
1 t	CURRY POWDER
2 T	CHUTNEY
2 T	WHITE SULTAN RAISINS
1/2 CUP	WATER CHESTNUTS (VERY THINLY SLICED)
1/4 CUP	BUTTER (MELTED)
1/4 CUP	CINNAMON-SUGAR

1. PREHEAT OVEN TO 450 DEGREES.
2. IN A BLENDER, BLEND TOGETHER CREAM CHEESE, COTTAGE CHEESE, CURRY POWDER AND CHUTNEY.
3. ADD RAISINS AND WATER CHESTNUTS.
4. FILL PAPAYA HALVES WITH MIXTURE. BAKE FOR 15 MINUTES.
5. SPRINKLE TOP WITH CINNAMON SUGAR AND POUR BUTTER OVER ALL.

PREPARATION: 5 MINUTES
BAKING: 15 MINUTES
SERVES: 2-6

Kapalua Bay Hotel

CHOCOLATE LAYER CAKE WITH GANACHE

3/4	CUP BUTTER	2	CUPS FLOUR (SIFTED)
3/4	CUP SUGAR	1	CUP HEAVY CREAM
6	EGGS (SEPARATED)	1/2	CUP EVAPORATED MILK
1	t VANILLA EXTRACT	1/4	CUP HONEY
5	OZ. SEMI-SWEET CHOCOLATE (MELTED AND COOLED)	11	OZ. SEMI-SWEET CHOCOLATE (CUT INTO SMALL CHUNKS)
		1	t INSTANT COFFEE

1. IN A MIXING BOWL CREAM BUTTER UNTIL FLUFFY. SLOWLY ADD SUGAR. BLEND.
2. BEAT IN EGG YOLKS ONE AT A TIME. ADD VANILLA.
3. IN A SEPARATE BOWL WHIP EGGS UNTIL WHITE AND STIFF. FOLD IN CHOCOLATE.
4. COMBINE TWO MIXTURES AND FOLD IN FLOUR UNTIL JUST BLENDED. DO NOT MIX TOO MUCH!
5. BAKE IN AN EIGHT INCH CAKE PAN AT 325 DEGREES FOR 45 MINUTES.
6. MEANWHILE IN A SMALL SAUCEPAN BRING WHIPPED CREAM, MILK, HONEY AND COFFEE TO A BOIL.
7. REMOVE FROM HEAT. ADD REMAINING CHOCOLATE. LET COOL.
8. SLOWLY WHIP HALF OF GANACHE (CHOCOLATE MIXTURE) UNTIL FLUFFY. RESERVE REMAINING HALF. CUT CAKE INTO 3 LAYERS AND FROST WITH WHIPPED GANACHE. REFRIGERATE FOR ONE HOUR.
9. USE REST OF GANACHE IN LIQUID FORM. POUR OVER CAKE AND LET COOL.

PREPARATION: 35-40 MINUTES   COOKING: 45 MINUTES

SERVES: 8

THE PLANTATION VERANDA
STEAK AND SEAFOOD
DINING 6:30-10:30 NIGHTLY
RESERVATIONS
669-5656
(JACKETS FOR MEN IN THE EVENING)

LOCATED IN KAPALUA BAY HOTEL
KAPALUA

The Veranda

The Veranda

LOCAL FISH BEURRE BLANC

2   SIX-OZ FILETS
3   OZ BUTTER (MELTED)
1|2 CUP BREAD CRUMBS
1|2 CUP WHITE WINE
2   OZ FRESH BUTTER
DASH OF WORCESTERSHIRE SAUCE
JUICE OF 1|2 LEMON
SALT AND PEPPER (TO TASTE)
CUCUMBER (GARNISH)

1. DIP FILETS IN MELTED BUTTER. DIP IN BREAD CRUMBS
2. POUR REMAINING MELTED BUTTER IN SKILLET AND SAUTÉ FILETS ON EACH SIDE UNTIL GOLDEN BROWN (3 MINUTES ON EACH SIDE).
3. REMOVE FILETS FROM SKILLET AND PLACE ON SERVING PLATTER.
4. IN SAME SKILLET ADD WINE AND REDUCE ONE-HALF.
5. THICKEN WITH BUTTER. SEASON WITH WORCESTERSHIRE SAUCE, LEMON, SALT AND PEPPER.
6. CUT CUCUMBER IN HALF MOONS AND GARNISH AROUND FILETS.
7. POUR SAUCE OVER ALL. SERVE WITH RICE.

PREPARATION: 5 MINUTES
COOKING: 10 MINUTES
SERVES: 2

The Veranda

MACADAMIA NUT SOUR CREAM PIE

1   9-INCH PASTRY CRUST (BAKED)
1-1/2 CUPS SOUR CREAM
3   EGG YOLKS
3/4 CUP SUGAR
2   T CORNSTARCH
1   t VANILLA
1   CUP BROKEN MACADAMIA NUTS (SLIGHTLY ROASTED)
JUICE OF 1/2 LEMON

1. IN A DOUBLE BROILER HEAT THE SOUR CREAM UNTIL HOT (DO NOT BOIL).
2. IN A MIXING BOWL BEAT EGG YOLKS LIGHTLY; STIR IN SUGAR AND CORNSTARCH.
3. INTO EGG MIXTURE GRADUALLY ADD THE HOT SOUR CREAM, STIRRING VIGOROUSLY.
4. PLACE MIXTURE BACK INTO PAN AND COOK OVER VERY LOW HEAT, STIRRING CONSTANTLY, FOR 15-20 MINUTES UNTIL THICK.
5. REMOVE MIXTURE FROM HEAT. ADD VANILLA AND COOL.
6. SQUEEZE LEMON OVER MACADAMIA NUTS AND INTO THE COOL MIXTURE. POUR EVERYTHING INTO BAKED PASTRY CRUST.
7. REFRIGERATE FOR A FEW HOURS BEFORE SERVING.

PREPARATION: 5-10 MINUTES
COOKING: 25-30 MINUTES
YIELD: ONE 9-INCH PIE

HONOLUA BAY

BLOWHOLE

BEYOND KAPALUA

PAST D. T. FLEMING BEACH PARK, ONE OF THE POPULAR RESORT BEACHES, IS MOKULEIA BEACH. THIS BEACH IS KNOWN AS SLAUGHTER HOUSE BEACH BY LOCALS BECAUSE THE OLD HONOLUA RANCH SLAUGHTERED CATTLE HERE AND ALLOWED THE WAVES BELOW DISPOSE OF THE WASTE! HONOLUA WAS THE ORIGINAL SIGHT OF THE HONOLUA RANCH (NOW IT IS A PINEAPPLE PLANTATION) BEGUN IN THE 1890S BY HENRY BALDWIN. NOW HONOLUA BAY IS NOTED FOR ITS EXCELLENT WAVES DURING WINTER MONTHS. ON THE RIGHT DAY THE WAVES CAN PRODUCE ONE OF THE BEST SURFING AREAS IN THE WORLD, AND ALMOST ALWAYS THE BEST SURFING ON MAUI! THERE IS OFTEN A CROWD ON THE CLIFFS ABOVE THE WAVES, WATCHING THE SURFERS.

PUNALAU AND HONOKOHAU ARE THE LAST SHORE-LINE AREAS WITH ANY SIZEABLE ACCUMULATIONS OF SAND. PUNALAU BEACH IS NOT VERY SAFE FOR SWIMMING OR SNORKELING ACTIVITIES BUT IS LOCALLY POPULAR FOR BEACHCOMBING AND PICNICKING. HONOKOHAU WAS ONCE A PROSPEROUS LITTLE SEASHORE SETTLE-

MENT, BUT NOW, SADLY, AS IT IS WITH ALMOST ALL OF THE LOCAL HAWAIIAN COMMUNITIES, FEW PEOPLE REMAIN HERE!

FROM HONOKOHAU BAY ON AROUND THE ISLAND TO WAIHEE IS A BEAUTIFUL AND NEARLY UNPOPULATED AREA OF HILLS AND CLIFFS, WITH SPECTACULAR VIEWS OF THE HEAVY SURF SMASHING INTO THE ROCKS BELOW...AND OF HALEAKALA. THERE IS A SLOW, ROUGH ROAD FOR ABOUT A MILE, BUT NOTHING DANGEROUS. THERE IS A "BLOWHOLE" TO SEE- IF YOU CAN FIND IT- AND THE SETTLEMENT AREA OF KAHAKULOA, A LITTLE FARMING-FISHING COMMUNITY.

KAHAKULOA VILLAGE

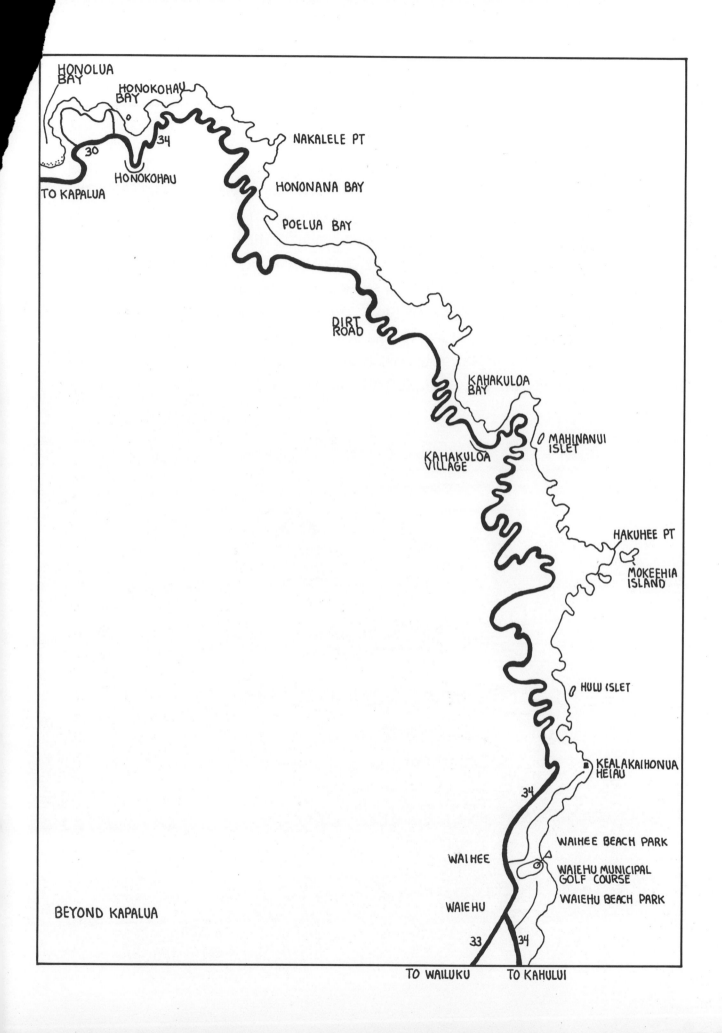

HONOLUA
BAY

HONOKOHAU
BAY

NAKALELE PT

30

34

HONOKOHAU

HONONANA BAY

TO KAPALUA

POELUA BAY

DIRT
ROAD

KAHAKULOA
BAY

MAHINANUI
ISLET

KAHAKULOA
VILLAGE

HAKUHEE PT

MOKEEHIA
ISLAND

HULU ISLET

KEALAKAIHONUA
HEIAU

34

WAIHEE BEACH PARK

WAIHEE

WAIEHU MUNICIPAL
GOLF COURSE

WAIEHU BEACH PARK

BEYOND KAPALUA

WAIEHU

33   34

TO WAILUKU   TO KAHULUI

ALOHA

BEYOND HAKUHE'E POINT THE ROAD DROPS DOWN TO WAIHEE AND SLOWLY
WENDS ITS WAY TO WAILUKU AND THE IAO VALLEY, WHERE OUR BOOK OF MAUI
TOUR BEGAN. NOW YOU SEE- AND FEEL- WHY MAUI IS SO SPECIAL! BEYOND
ITS ENDLESS BEAUTY IS A CHARM THAT BRINGS JOY TO THE HEART AND A WAY
OF LIFE THAT SOOTHES THE VERY SOUL! MAUI IS THE ESSENCE OF HAWAII. AS
YOU HAVE SEEN, IT IS NOT A LARGE ISLAND... AND YET MAUI IS MANY DISTINCT
AND COMPLEX WORLDS: THE WONDER OF IAO, THE SPECTACLE OF
HALEAKALA, THE GARDENS OF KULA, THE BUSY RESORT LIFE OF KAANAPALI,
THE ELEGANCE OF KAPALUA AND WAILEA, THE LOCAL LIFE OF WAILUKU,
THE BEAUTY OF HANA! MAUI OFFERS SO MUCH! MAY YOU REMEMBER
US FONDLY! MAY YOU OFTEN RETURN TO US!

HAKUHE'E
POINT